C000271597

THE RICH DESIGNS OF

Clarice Cliff

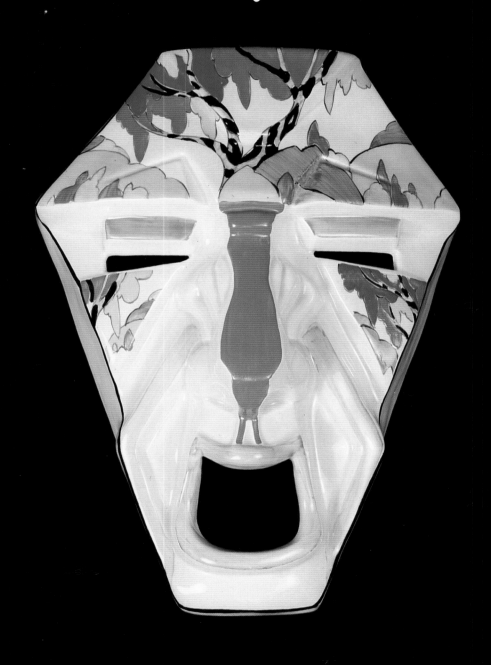

THIS BOOK IS DEDICATED TO
Len Griffin and the Bizarre Girls

THE RICH
DESIGNS OF

Clarice
Cliff

RICHARD GREEN
AND DES JONES

— PUBLISHED BY —

RICH DESIGNS

BOOK DESIGNED BY

JACK GERTSON

First published in Great Britain, November 1995 by:
Rich Designs Limited,
Unit 3, 7A Waterloo Industrial Estate,
Bidford-on-Avon,
Warwickshire B50 4JN
01789 772111

ISBN 0 9526354 1 0

All rights reserved. No part of this publication may be produced, stored in a retrieval system, or transmitted, in any form or by any means, electronic, mechanical, photocopying, recording or otherwise without the prior permission of the publishers.

This book is sold subject to the condition that it shall not, by way of trade or otherwise, be lent, re-sold, hired out or otherwise circulated without the publisher's prior consent in any form of binding or cover other than that in which it is published and without a similar condition including this condition being imposed on the subsequent purchaser.

© Text, captions and photographs:
  Rich Designs Limited 1995

Book design and print production:
Jack Gertson (0181-554 4366)

Artwork originated and text set in Janson on Apple Macintosh by:
Ian Christmas

Colour origination and print:
Garden House Press Limited,
Perivale UB6 7LA England

Text paper:
150gsm Highland Velvet PRO
(Hannoart Top Matt)
Manufactured by:
Hannover Papier
(a member of Sappi Europe)
and supplied by:
McNaughton Publishing
Papers Limited

Bound by:
Hunter & Foulis Limited,
Edinburgh EH7 4NP Scotland

ACKNOWLEDGEMENTS

For over ten years Len Griffin's dedicated research has informed and introduced many people to the life and work of Clarice Cliff.

The regular contact with 'his' *Bizarre* Girls and commitment to the Clarice Cliff Collectors Club, which he formed, has made him one of the leading authorities on the subject.

Without his tenacity, little would have been written about Clarice Cliff and even less would have been known.

Without his major contribution *The Rich Designs of Clarice Cliff* would not have been written.

All the original photographs in this book were taken by Richard Green with Chris Metcalf's assistance.

We would also like to thank the following people for their invaluable help:

> Eric Grindley
> Jim Hall and Marjory Higginson
> Doreen Jenkins
> Chris Metcalf
> Mike Slaney

Finally, our special thanks to Jack Gertson for taking our numerous computer disks, manuscripts and photographs and creating this book.

Page 1:
Honolulu
See page 100.

Page 3:
Inspiration Lily
1929-1930
Pink lilies against a blue *Inspiration* ground, with black leaves. Occasionally has a red glaze effect to the base.
★★★★££££

Opposite page:
A selection of single and double *Yo Yo* vases in various patterns.

Top:
Len Griffin with some of Clarice's original *Bizarre* Girls at a 1987 re-union.
Seated left to right.
Eileen Tharme, Nellie Webb, Winnie Pound, Marjory Higginson, Doris Johnson, Nora Dabbs and Rene Dale.
Standing left to right.
May Booth, Phyllis Tharme, Ivy Stringer, Jessie McKenzie, Vera Hollins (partly hidden), Elsie Nixon, Kathy Keeling, Cissy Rhodes, Annie Beresford and Gladys Baggaley.

Thanks to the following who kindly allowed us to photograph their collections.

Jill Bailey
Michael and Helen Bailey
Hayley and Andrew Ball
Paul and Sue Bell
Jerry Bloomfield
Jean Broadbent
Joan Burton
Gavin Casey
Greg and Julie Chetland
Brian Clissold
Mr J. Cook
Mrs M. Crossley
Cathy and Chris Cutting
Johnathan Daltrey and Alan Brooks
Ian Dredge
Ted Elliot
Peter Ford
J. and C. Foster
Jill and Jack Gertson
David and Barbara Gilfillan
Richard and Kathy Green
Ricki Grey
Len Griffin
Alistair and Elizabeth Haldane
Pam and Graham Harding
Muir Hewitt
Mark Higgin
Mike Hogger
Dave and Sue Holder
Phil Holden
Ian Holmes
Julian Homer
Des Jones
Marshall Kostka
David Latham
Chris Metcalf
Steve and Lavinia Metcalf
Andrew Muir
Sylvia and Martin Patrick
Maria Pedro
Freda Pilz
David Pratt
Edward Prior
John and Lynda Pritchard
Chris Radford
Susan W. Robertson
James Roe
Dave and Sally Sands
John and Jean Saunders
Mike Slaney
Derek and Irene Smith
John Smith
Nicholas Stockton
Bob and Chris Thompson
Ian and Annie Tickler
Leslie and Martin Totty
Nigel Underwood
Sue and George Walters
Robin Willets

Both Christies/South Kensington and the Stoke Library and Museum also helped by providing some photographs.

Apples

PATTERN INDEX	8
INTRODUCTION	11
FINDING YOUR PATTERN	15
CHAPTER ONE: 1916-1927 Before Bizarre	19
CHAPTER TWO: 1928 The begining of Bizarre	28
CHAPTER THREE: 1929 New shapes and glazes	44
CHAPTER FOUR: 1930 A runaway success	72
CHAPTER FIVE: 1931 The pace continues	104
CHAPTER SIX: 1932 Cruising along	130
CHAPTER SEVEN: 1933 An interruption	150
CHAPTER EIGHT: 1934 A creative dilution	172
CHAPTER NINE: 1935 The magic fades?	186
CHAPTER TEN: 1936-1972 After Bizarre	196
CHAPTER ELEVEN: 1973 The collectors	216
FURTHER READING	232

BOLD PAGE NUMBERS INDICATE
THE PATTERN IS ILLUSTRATED

Acacia 230
Acorn 34, **35**
Age of Jazz figures 42, **42**
Alton 12, **14**
Amberose 34, **35**
Anemone 176, **176**
Apples 6, 11
Arabesque 44, **45**
Archaic **10, 11**
Arizona 230
Artists In Industry 16, **17**
Aura 230
Aurea 16, **17**
Autumn 22, **22, 23, 26, 29**
Autumn Crocus 80, **81**
Avignon 12, **13**
Avon 32, **32**

Bamboo 36, **36**
Batanga 230
Beach Ball 38, **38**
Beechwood 230
Bermuda 38, **38**
Berries 20, **21**
Bignou 40, **40**
Bird of Paradise 26, **27**
Bizarre 24, **25**
Blossom 44, **44**
Blue Crocus 82, **82**
Blue Daisy 46, **46**
Blue-Eyed Marigolds 50, **50**
Blue Firs 30, **30**
Blue Heaven 52, **52**
Blue Ribbon 56, **56**
Blueberry Tree 56, **56**
Blue 'W' 30, **31**
Bobbins 54, **54**
Bowling **64**, 65
Braidwood 230
Branch & Squares **64**, 65
Bridgwater 32, **33**
Brookfields 34, **35**
Broth 36, **37**
Brunella 72, **72**
Buttercup 72, **72**
Butterfly 56, **56**

Cabbage Flower 76, **76**
Café 60, **61**
Cafe-au-Lait 38, **39**
Canterbury Bells 40, **41**
Car & Skyscraper 68, **68**
Capri 60, **60**
Caprice 62, **62**
Caravan 42, **43**
Carpet 46, **47**
Castellated Circle 48, **49**
Celtic Harvest 62, **62**, 223, **223**
Chalet **64**, 65
Cherry 66, **66**
Cherry Blossom 76, **76**
Cherry Tree 230
Chestnut 230
Chintz 50, **51**
Christine 78, **78**
Circle Tree 52, **53**
Circles & Squares 70, **70**
Clematis 230

Clouvre 18, 68, **68**
Clovelly 74, **74**
Coastal Oak 78, **78**
Comets 54, **55**
Coral Firs 56, **57**
Cornwall 230
Cowslip 58, **59**
Crab Apple 222, **222**
Crayon Scenes 62, **63**
Crazy Paving 222, **222**
Crepe de Chine 76, **76**
Crest 80. **80**
Crocus 80
Cruiseware 230
Cubist 66, **67**

Damask Rose 84, **84**
Delecia 92, **92**
Delecia Citrus 86, **86**
Delecia Daisy 92, **92**
Delecia Pansies 92, **92**
Delecia Peaches 230
Delecia Poppy 92, **92**
Devon 88, **88**
Diamonds 68, **69**
Dijon 230
Dolphins 230
Dore 88, **88**
Double 'V' 70, **71**
Dryday 94, 95

Eating Apples 94, 95
Eden **94**, 95
Elizabethan Cottage 96, **96**
Erin 98, **98**
Etna 72, **73**
Exotic 230

Farmhouse 76, **77**
Feather & Leaves 132, **132**
Ferndale 106, **106**
Flora 106, **106**
Floreat 98, **98**
Florida 230
Flower Music 100, **100**
Flower & Squares 106, **106**
Flower Wave 104, **104**
Foam 230
Football 90, **91**
Forest Glen 82, **83**
Forest Leaves 230
Fragrance 84, **85**
Fruit 110, **110**
Fruitburst 108, **108**
Fuchsia 230
Full Circle 108, **108**

Gallion 230
Garden 86, **87**
Gardenia 88, **89**
Garland 110, **110**
Gayday 78, **79**
Geometric Flowers 112, **112**
Gibraltar **93**, 95
Gloria 116, **116**
Gloria Crocus 230
Golden Oranges 230
Goldstone 122, **122**
Gordon 230
Green Firs 96, **97**
Green House 98, **99**
Grill 230

Hawthorn 230
Hello 230
Hollyhocks 116, **116**
Hollyrose 116, **116**
Honeydew 114, **114**
Honiton **124**, 125
Honolulu 1, 100, **101**
House & Bridge 102, **103**
Hydrangea 118, **118**

Idyll 104, **105**
Indian Summer 230
Industry 122, **122**
Inspiration Caprice 74, **75**
Inspiration Delphinium 230
Inspiration Embossed 230
Inspiration Garden 230
Inspiration Knight Errant 110, **111**
Inspiration Lily 3, 5
Inspiration Nasturtium 230
Inspiration Rose 74, **75**
Islands **124**, 125

Jagged Flower 230
Japan 108, **109**

Kandina 122, **122**
Kang 230
Kelverne **124**, 125
Kensington 230
Kew 116, **117**
Keyhole 132, **132**
Killarney 136, **136**

Latona Aztec 230
Latona Blossom 231
Latona Bouquet 114, **115**
Latona Brown 231
Latona Cartoon Flowers 231

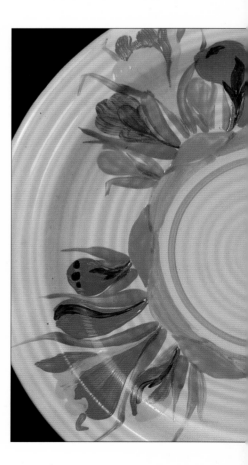

Latona Dahlia 112, **113**
Latona Flowerheads 114, **115**
Latona Geometric 231
Latona Knight Errant 231
Latona Mushroom 114, **115**
Latona Red Roses 114, **115**
Latona Thistle 114, **115**
Latona Tree 114, **115**
Latona Stained Glass 231
Leaf Tree 136, **136**
Le Bon Dieu 134, **134**
Liberty 138, **138**
Lightning 118, **119**
Lily 128, **128**
Limberlost 106 **107**
Line Jazz 122, **123**
Lisbon 128, **128**
Lodore 138, **138**
London 130, **130**
Lorna 134, **134**
Lucerne 126, **127, 129**
Lugano 130, **131, 133**
Lupin **154**, 155
Luxor 134, **135**
Lydiat 136, **136**

Mango 222, **222**
Marguerite 140, **140**
Marigold 136, **137**
Marlow 223, **223**
May Avenue 138, **139**
May Blossom **154**, 155
Melon **140**, 142, **142, 143**
Milano 231
Moderne 166, **166**
Mondrian 144, **145**
Monsoon 146, **147**
Moonflower 146, **146**
Moonlight 148, **148**

Morning 231
Morocco 152, **152**
Moselle 152, **152**
Mountain 140, **141**
Mowcop 166, **166**
My Garden 168, **168**

Napoli 168, **168**
Nasturtium 148, **149**
Nemesia 174, **174**
New Flag 174, **174**
Newlyn 82, **83**
Newport **154**, 155
Nuage 156, **156**

Oasis 144, **144**
Opalesque Stencil Deer 158, **158**
Ophelia 231
Orange Battle 150, **151**
Orange/Blue Squares 158, **158**
Orange House 152, **153**
Orange Roof Cottage 156, **157**,
222, **222**
Orange 'V' 160, **160**
Oranges 158, **159**
Oranges & Lemons 160, **161**

Palermo 162, **163**
Palm 231
Parrot Tulip 164, **164**
Passion Fruit 176, **176**
Patina Blue Firs 231
Patina Coastal 231
Patina Country 231
Patina Daisy 231
Patina Tree 164, **166**
Pebbles 170, **170**
Persian (Inspiration) 120, **121**
Persian (Original) 164, **165**
Peter Pan Crocus 32, **32**
Petunia 40, **41**
Picasso Flower 166, **167**, 223, **223**
Piccadilly 231
Pine Grove **184**, 185
Pink Pearls **184**, 185
Pink Roof Cottage 170, **170**
Pink Tree 172, **172**
Poplar 168, **169**
Posy 222, **222**
Propeller 170, **171**
Purple Crocus 82, **82**

Raffia 231
Rainbow 231
Ravel 176, **176**
Red Roofs 172, **173**
Red Tree 174, **175**
Red Tulip 178, **178**
Regatta 231
Reverie 231
Rhodanthe **177**, 178
Rudyard 178, **179**

Sand Flower 222, **222**
Sandon 84, **85**
Scarlet Flower 223, **223**
Scraphito 180, **180**
Secrets 180, **181**
Shark's Teeth **192**, 193
Silver Birch **192**, 193
Sliced Circle 182, **183**
Sliced Fruit 182, **182**

Solitude 186, **187**
Solomon's Seal **184**, 185
Spire 204, **204**
Spring Crocus 231
Springtime 231
Stile & Trees 186, **186**
Stroud **206**, 207
Summer 231
Summer Crocus 8 & **9**, 9
Summerhouse 212, **213**
Sunburst 204, **205**
Sundew 114, **114**
Sungay 78, **79**
Sungleam Crocus 80, **80**
Sungold 188, **188**
Sunray 208, **209**
Sunray Leaves 188, **188**
Sunrise 194, **194**
Sunshine **192**, 193
Sunspots 202, **203**
Swirls 198, **199**

Tahiti 231
Taormina 202, **202**
Tartan 196, **196**
Tartan Poppy 198, **198**
Tennis 200, **201**
Tibetan 231
Trallee **85**, 86
Tree 198, **198**
Trees & House **189**, 190, **190**,
191, 195
Trent **206**, 207
Tulips 200, **200**
Twig 231
Twin Peaks 210, **211**

Umbrellas 204, **204**
Umbrellas & Rain **206**, 207

Vienna 231
Viscaria 16, **17**

Water Lily 223, **223**
Watermill **220**, 221
Wax Flower 208, **208**
Wheat 231
Windbells 214. **215**
Windflowers 210, **211**
Windmill 216. **217**
Windows 231
Winsome **220**, 221
Woman's Journal 210, **210**
Woodland 212, **212**

Xanthic 216, **216**
Xavier 218, **218**

Yellow Orchid 231
Yellow Rose 223, **223**
Yoo Hoo 231
Yuan 231
Yugoslavian Dancers 218, **219**

Zap **220**, 221

This page:
Summer Crocus
Bizarre
1934
Autumn Crocus flowers on a green glaze.
★★★★£

INTRODUCTION

by Leonard Griffin

All Clarice Cliff collectors are inevitably fascinated by this determined yet mysterious woman. Even if she had not covered them with so much jazzy colour, just the shapes of her teapots, vases and fancies are themselves a celebration of imagination let loose. Her designs embrace the shapes they were made for.

The most commercial ware is found in the outlined pieces, generally in brown or black, with their strident orange, green, blues, yellows; *Melon*, *Sunray* or *Blue 'W'* fall in this category. The rarer but equally efficient *Tennis* and *Carpet* were executed freehand, and are unique in their "shock" impact. The slightly less typical but rainbowesque *Appliqué* designs, show Clarice's bravest use of blocks of colour en-masse.

Her unique gift was in taking parts of the English countryside and turning them into homely scenes, that appealed because of the security offered by their cartoon-like trees and cottages. Amongst these *Autumn*, *Summerhouse*, *Trees & House*, *Secrets*, *Coral & Blue Firs* have an on-going appeal. The palette of sugary pastels of pink, blue and lilac for *Gibralt*; *Pink Roof Cottage* and *Pastel Melon*, was in complete contrast to the orange-dominated designs. It was clearly chosen to cater for a customer with different tastes in 1932, and still does today.

Her understanding of commercial appeal was testified to in her *My Garden* ware with its raised flowers, and the etched designs such as *Rhodanthe* that sold in thousands in the Thirties. Their popularity when issued makes them more accessible today than the brighter and brasher landscapes or geometrics, whose small sales originally make them expensive now. *Rhodanthe* has often been the first design to attract new collectors to Cliff. It is almost like finding your front door on a completely strange and unknown house: you approach it, recognise something, and go in to discover a whole new world....

As more and more collectors have become intrigued by the work of Clarice Cliff, in turn a greater variety of her designs and shapes have become collectable. The more affordable and accessible ware produced after 1936 is the attention of many more collectors now than in the mid -Eighties.

Since many pieces of her post-war ware are still in the homes of the original purchasers, we will not know for some time if yet another generation of collectors will rise up who will find her *Novota* range or the hand-painted ware in the 1953 series 7722 to 7747 desirable. They have the magic *Clarice Cliff* mark, and as functional ware, in a durable form they might be both chic, and cheap, to young couples rejecting expensive contemporary tableware in the twenty-first century.

We know that Clarice Cliff wanted to be a sculptress in 1926, and her achievements in the following ten years were something she could not have foreseen or planned. The faith of Colley Shorter in her, meant she had the chance to experiment with ceramic shapes in a way no one else was able to. Her successes such as the *Conical* teapot, the *Yo Yo* vase, the *Age of Jazz* figures,

Page 6:
Apples
Fantasque
1931-1932
Stylised apples and grapes in natural colours, but with pink, yellow and orange segmented leaves, and black oblongs resembling piano notes. Referred to as *New Fruit* in the archives.
★★★★££££

Opposite:
Archaic
Bizarre
1929-1930
Vases shaped as classical columns, copied from *The Grammar of Ornament* by Owen Jones as were the designs. Produced with a black print which was then enamelled. The shapes were numbers 372 to 377, and since the stock of glost ware was not used up, they were later utilised for standard designs.
★★★★★£££££

Page 7:
Clarice Cliff pictured in a rare close-up in 1932, wearing a *Liberty* scarf.

and the endless vases easily outweigh the aberrations. The frankly, ugly, *Le Bon Dieu* ware and the unsuccessful *Goldstone* body were however innovations that were simply not commercially viable at the time. The speckled *Goldstone* ware would have been a big success in the Seventies in Britain when *Midwinter's* Stonehenge ware, with its flecked surface was popular!

Clarice Cliff copied shapes by Josef Hoffmann for a cigarette and match holder, and her *Biarritz* tureen. She plagiarised Modigliani for *May Avenue*. However, to translate this into her being a follower of the *Wiener Werkstätte* or of colourist painters does not give us a true picture of her artistic gifts. She was not a high-brow academic, but an artist with an open attitude, and a thirst to create new ceramics. Almost at the same time as she was using Hoffmann's shapes she was dreaming up her very English *My Garden* ware, which owed nothing to Austrian design. Whilst *My Garden* has not proved majorly collectable in the last twenty years, its real significance is that it was desirable for buyers of ceramics in Britain between 1934 and 1939. As an Industrial designer Clarice Cliff excelled at understanding public taste, and subliminally introduced her customers to styles, movement and shapes they would otherwise have been unaware of.

Clarice was just as happy with *My Garden* as she was with her *Age of Jazz*. Her task was to supply Colley Shorter with as many different and varied design and shape ideas as she could. How the public responded to these was his concern. She had an open-attitude to design, as even when she was thirty-five she still seemed keen to embrace new ideas, she did not exclude any shape, colour or texture from her work because of any self-imposed parameters.

Clarice Cliff's fancies were often art translated into a form acceptable by everyone. And this was her gift, she was an ordinary woman with the ability to see what others could not, and the skill to make everyday objects art. That she was ahead of her time is certainly true, and our inability to be able to categorise her work is not a fault in her. She had many influences, but dissolved these into a single-minded passion to create and design ceramics covering a large cross-section of taste.

Clarice Cliff was equally at ease designing traditional floral ware, as she was at modelling outlandish vase shapes, and this confuses those who try to classify her. An Art Deco designer would not model vases with embossed flowers, an Art Nouveau designer would never base a design on a geometric form, and a follower of the principles of Cubism would never produce landscapes of trees and cottages. Clarice Cliff was each of these, but not in a purist sense, she simply recognised the strengths of each movement, and embraced them temporarily to fuel her vivid and open imagination. She felt no qualms about producing her revolutionary *Conical* teapot in her best selling *Crocus* design or drowning a geometrically shaped vase in the "runnings" of her *Delecia* decoration.

Clarice Cliff's unique ability was that unlike all the other designers in the Thirties she was not influenced by artistic misconceptions or snobbery. She did not care if academics did not take her work seriously. She saw no barriers between styles, and pulled down technical barriers at her factory. In 1931 when everyone else ignored Art Nouveau, she returned to its principles for her *Daffodil* shape ware. She was not trying to convey her own image in her work, but a mass of images that she named extremely well - *Bizarre*.

"*Having a little fun at my work does not make me any less of an artist, and people who appreciate truly beautiful and original creations in pottery are not frightened by innocent tomfoolery!*"

Page 14:
Alton
Bizarre
1934
Distant castle turrets partly hidden by a bushy hillside with colourful flowers in the foreground: named after Alton Towers in Staffordshire: brush outline.
Colourways:
Brown or Green ★★★£££
Orange ★★★★★£££

Opposite:
Avignon
Appliqué
1930-1931
A blue bridge over a lake in an ornamental garden under an orange sky.
Two examples known with coral red sky.
★★★★★£££££

Alton

FINDING YOUR PATTERN

If you know the name of your pattern the Pattern Index on pages 8 and 9 will identify the pages that you require.

If the pattern name is unknown to you then it can be found by studying the illustrations and descriptions.

Each design name is followed by the range name; the approximate dates of production; a brief description and a rarity and value guide if appropriate.

Where an alternate colourway exists this will also be indicated.

PATTERN NAMES

The pattern names used contain a mixture of original factory names plus those given when the original name is unknown. Many given names are now universally accepted. Attributed pattern names that are falling out of use, or have been replaced with the correct factory name, follow in brackets after the main name.

DESIGN RANGES

Most standard hand-painted designs are part of a range and this is shown after the pattern name. Some examples of the stamps applied to the ware are illustrated below and the design ranges are described on the right:

Bizarre
1928-1936
Clarice's first and most successful range, covering all patterns from early geometrics to landscapes.

Appliqué
1930-1931
Clarice's most colourful ware, using more expensive enamels than *Bizarre* or *Fantasque*, and produced using Indian ink outlining.

Fantasque
1929-1934
This was a range of new hand painted designs to be sold alongside *Bizarre*. These were slightly more expensive than the standard *Bizarre* range but many were inadvertently only marked *Bizarre* during this busy period.

Inspiration
1929-1930
A range produced with the glaze being the decoration. Blue, pink, purple and brown metallic oxide glazes painted onto the biscuit ware then fired at higher temperatures than *Bizarre*.

Latona
1929-1932
A milky coloured glaze introduced in 1929. Designs were painted freehand.

Clarice Cliff
1936-1963
Most of the output of the factory had this stamp from the end of 1936.

DECORATION STYLES

The vast majority of Clarice Cliff ware was produced with a brush outline. All designs using other techniques have brief details of the style, for instance; pen outline, freehand, printed outline, underglaze decoration, etched and runnings.

Glossary of Decoration Styles

Brush Outline
1927 onwards
The design is painted as an outline in a single colour and the enamels have been painted within these lines.
Examples include Original Bizarre, Autumn, Summerhouse, Trees & House and House & Bridge.

Pen Outline
1933 onwards
The design is painted with a very fine outline in a single colour with a pen and the enamels have been painted within these.
Examples include Coral Firs, Blue Firs, Japan and Bridgwater.

Freehand
1928 onwards
There is no outline, all the elements have been painted freehand in medium or thick brush strokes, except for perhaps some fine detail such as the thin leaves on *Crocus* or the "net" effect on *Tennis*.
Examples include Crocus, Gayday, Ravel, Carpet, Tennis, Sunspots and most Latona designs.

Indian Ink Freehand
1930-1933
Used exclusively for *Appliqué* designs, these pieces were originally produced as an Indian ink outline, and then the colours added between these. When fired the Indian ink lining burns away leaving blocks of solid colour with no lining. A few lines were subsequently added for delineating a feature, as on the building walls in *Lugano*.
Examples include Lucerne, Windmill and Red Tree.

Etched
1934 onwards
Freehand decoration where adjacent colours are etched into each other to give a shading effect between them.
Examples include Rhodanthe, Trallee and Sandon.

Embossed Freehand
1930 onwards
The ware has a modelled surface where all or part of the colour is painted within these pre-determined limits.
Examples include Scraphito, My Garden, Raffia and Corncob.

Under Glaze Decoration
1930-1931
The colour is applied to the biscuit ware, with the glaze then added over it.
Examples include Gloria.

High-Fired Designs
1929-1935
Coloured glazes applied in a liquid state by the paintresses so they are both the glaze and design.
Examples include Inspiration and Opalesque.

Surface Ornamentation
1930-1933
Ware is decorated initially in an all-over effect, and the design is then painted on top of this.
Examples include Cafe-au-Lait and Patina.

Runnings
1929-1937
Enamel colours applied all over or on just part of the ware in a liquid state to run over it.
Examples include Delecia, Pansies and Forest Glen.

Printed Outline
1930-1932
A print is applied to the ware, which is then enamelled and banded as normal. These can be distinguished by their regular line, plus the fact that each piece looks very similar.
Examples include Solomon's Seal, Woodland, Nemesia and Sunshine.

Some designs incorporated elements of the above, for instance *Taormina* has a pen outline combined with etched detail for the tree, *Forest Glen* combines pen outline with both runnings and etching.

RARITY AND VALUE

At the end of most descriptions, symbols give an indication of the rarity and value of the pattern.

Rarity definitions

★★★★★	Known from less than 10 examples at present.
★★★★	Known from less than 100 examples at present.
★★★	Fairly difficult to find.
★★	Fairly easy to find.
★	Easy to find.

Value definitions

££££££	A design which always sells at a high price.
££££	A design which sells at a medium to high price.
£££	A design which sells at a medium price.
££	An inexpensive to medium priced design.
£	An inexpensive design.

When valuing a piece the shape on which the design is painted has a big impact on the value. An 'ordinary' design on a *Yo Yo* vase will therefore be expensive.

Top:
Artists In Industry
1932-1934
The series of tableware designs produced by noted Thirties artists, produced as part of the *Art In Industry* project, launched in 1932 and completed in late 1934. Artists who contributed included Angelica Bell, Vanessa Bell, Freda Beardmore, Frank Brangwyn, John Armstrong, Duncan Grant, Eva Crofts (teaset opposite), Laura Knight, Ann Riach, John Everett, Barbara Hepworth, Dod Proctor, Ernest Proctor, Albert Rutherston, Paul Nash, Ben Nicholson, Milner Gray, Graham Sutherland, Moira Forsyth, W. P. Robbins, Billie Walters, Alan Walton, Michael Wellmer, Gordon Foysyth and Thomas Acland Fennemore, whose ware was signed Thomas Acland.

Bottom:
Aurea
Bizarre
1934-1937
The etched *Rhodanthe* design in alternative colourways.
Green ★★£
Blue ★★★£
See also *Rhodanthe* and *Viscaria*.

Bottom:
Viscaria
Bizarre
1934-1936
Tall etched flowers in pink, on sinuous green stems painted freehand.
★★£
See also *Rhodanthe* and *Aurea*.

CHAPTER I

1916-1927

BEFORE BIZARRE

Using the name Clarice Cliff to launch brightly coloured, imaginatively shaped ceramics today might not be out of the ordinary. In 1928 it was *Bizarre*. Clarice was just one of thousands of young women earning a meagre and erratic income at one of the hundreds of pot banks in the area of Staffordshire known as the Potteries.

In the middle of the Great War, Clarice Cliff joined the A. J. Wilkinson factory near Burslem. In 1916 as an apprentice lithographer she could not afford an apron for her first day at work. In contrast by 1930 she was Art Director of a pottery solely producing her designs and shapes, which were sold throughout the world.

As a lithographer she had spent each day applying prints to ware of traditional scenes. As a designer she used the manufacturing abilities of hundreds of workers, and supervised sixty hand-paintresses who skilfully executed her designs onto ware in hundreds of different shapes.

The move from lithographer to designer was not a simple one, as in 1916 there was no precedent for a young woman to achieve this role in Stoke-on-Trent. The industry was extremely traditional, and even the factories who employed designers, rarely let these men be credited for their work. How was it then that just twelve years after she started, every piece of ware she issued was marked *Bizarre by Clarice Cliff*? The answer to that question is complex, and is one of the reasons why a mystique grew around Clarice and her pottery in the Thirties; a mystique that still exists today.

Clarice was gradually given more and more responsibility. She kept the pattern books, where in her strong stylish handwriting she detailed the processes to produce the ware of the two chief designers, Fred Ridgway and John Butler.

A. J. Wilkinson had established an excellent reputation for the quality of its earthenware, but had never been noted for the artistry of its designs. Arthur Shorter, the owner since 1894, had two sons. His eldest, Arthur Colley Austin Shorter, was known as Colley Shorter, or "Mr. Colley" to his workers. He left school aged 16 in 1898 and became a salesman for Wilkinson's. The youngest son, Guy, left school in 1900 and went as a manager to the original family factory, Shorter & Sons in Copeland Street.

By 1920 Colley and Guy Shorter were doing so well that they took advantage of the opportunity to buy the adjoining Newport Pottery. This poorly run potbank had never been able to equal the quality of Wilkinson's earthenware, but they took it over and introduced their methods.

Unaware of the significance Newport Pottery would play in her life, Clarice spent her first few years at Wilkinson's learning more and more about the production and decoration processes. In 1919 she befriended Reg Lamb, a worker from the clay end, who supplied her with lumps of expensive modelling clays. She used these to produce figures, both at the factory after work, and at home in Tunstall at the weekend. She had been inspired by watching the experienced modellers and tried to teach herself sculpting, but her efforts were crude.

The girls who worked with Clarice at this time recalled that she was never really one of them. When they left to go home Clarice often stayed behind, modelling clay, or wandering from shop to shop; she regarded her work as more than a job. Her sister Ethel later summed it up when she said, "Clarice was never interested in going dancing like the rest of us, her work always came first."

It is easy to envisage the Twenties as the Jazz Age. Everyone wanted to have fun after the "war to end all wars". There were motor cars, cocktails, and Cole Porter songs. For the first time women were emancipated and able to enjoy themselves as equals to

Opposite:
Clouvre
See page 68.

men. It was the first decade when women were able to vote, but the reality was that although they had won this right in 1918, it was only for women over thirty years of age until 1928. Clarice was therefore excluded from voting from 1918 to 1928, so she would have been keenly aware that women still did not have full equality.

Unlike her four sisters, Sara, Hannah, Dorothy and Ethel, Clarice had a goal, and was to achieve it. By the mid-Twenties, Dorothy, or Dolly as she was known, was working at Wilkinson's where she was in charge of apprentices in a small shop producing traditional hand-painted ware. However, Dolly did not aspire to design, and lived for her life as a dancer after work.

It was on one of her jaunts round the factory after work that Clarice picked up a vase in a decorating shop and started painting a butterfly. The story goes that Jack Walker the work's manager was impressed by what he saw. However, it is more likely that her enthusiasm and hard work over a long period drew Walker's attention to her potential, which in turn led Mr. Colley to become aware of her. Of all the influences in her life, Colley Shorter was to be the most important, both professionally and personally.

Throughout the Twenties Colley Shorter cultivated an overseas dealer network in Australia, New Zealand, South Africa and South America. Travel to these countries was a long and difficult process, but he spent weeks on such trips, the personal contact must have been a key factor in securing overseas orders. Consignments were generally sent twice a year, the majority of the ware being the more prestigious lines that gave the most profit.

The International Exhibition of Modern Decorative and Industrial Art was held in Paris in 1925. Decades later an abbreviation from the original French title, *Exposition des Arts Décoratifs et Industriel* gave writers the term Art Deco. This neatly classified the period after Art Nouveau with a name that followed the same style. Every pottery in Stoke-on-Trent was influenced in some way by the exhibition, but the results took some time to appear, and the majority did not really capture the spirit of Art Deco. Many influential figures in the Potteries at this time did not realise the significance of the new movement and disparagingly referred to it as "Jazz Modern". Gordon Forsyth, superintendent of the Schools of Art in the area preached that, "It was only through Art that the pottery industry would gain fresh ground". This led to responses from various figures in the industry including Cyril Carter of Carter, Stabler & Adam's (later Poole) Pottery. He wrote to the *Pottery Gazette & Glass Trade Review* "If Mr. Forsyth can induce us to think a little less about Art as a name and a little more about making honest pottery, fitting in every way for the purpose for which it is made, one cannot help feeling we shall be moving in the right direction."

Clarice Cliff was oblivious to these exchanges. From her early days purloining modelling clays, to the patterns she painted with bare fingers in wet plaster long after she retired, Clarice was not to conform to anyone's philosophy.

Clarice's attitude meant that she was generally respected by her paintresses, but handled warily by the male-dominated departments of the factory. An encounter with Clarice generally resulted in her getting her own way. This is fortunate as without her obstinance there would be no *Conical* bowls, no *Stamford* teapots, no *Age of Jazz* figures. She was a one-off who achieved what she did by ignoring boundaries. Clarice created a role for herself that in the second half of the century would have made her a career woman, but in 1929 at least, made her, "That bloody woman!"

How did Clarice Cliff achieve what she did? Initially, slowly. Although we can trace *Bizarre* back to the advent of Art Deco, that style was itself fuelled by a craze for things Egyptian, that followed the opening of Tutankhamen's tomb in 1923. The genesis of what was to become *Bizarre* happened between 1924 and 1927. Apart from her work with Butler and Ridgway, Clarice continued her modelling and, we know from extant examples that the workers on the bottle-ovens fired her solid clay figures. These crudely modelled pieces were hand-painted, on-glaze, in enamel colours.

It may be that Clarice's enthusiasm for modelling was noticed by Colley Shorter, as the 1925 and 1926 prototype models led to ware that was actually issued. A stylised *Duck* figure was used as a bookend, as was a production version of the *Arab* figure. Clarice soon elaborated on the original version of this to produce a more stylised one,

Opposite:
Berries
Fantasque
1930-1932
Red and orange berries, blue and purple leaves, with green and yellow oblongs.
★★★££££

an amorous pair were called *Friday Night Ducks*. One of her best pieces from this time was the *Girl* candlestick, featuring a woman kneeling in a flowing dress, holding a bowl of flowers aloft, which was the candle's sconce. Another shape that was to be used extensively during the *Bizarre* years appeared at this time, the *Beehive* honeypot, with a colourful bee forming the handle on its lid. The *Laughing Cat* figure was based on a larger original designed for Wilkinson's by Louis Wain in the mid-Twenties, Clarice modelled a small version which was normally decorated in spots. Her *Viking Boat* flower holder appeared in 1927, so along with her work as a hand-paintress Clarice was now acting as a modeller.

Colley Shorter was clearly impressed by the pieces Clarice made, and as was the case with modellers in the works, he arranged for her to have her own studio. Newport Pottery had spare accommodation and he arranged for her to be based there. Subsequent events perhaps showed that he wanted Clarice to be away from the busy atmosphere at Wilkinson's. She became remote from the other workers who noticed that Mr. Colley was treating her differently; his manner with them was often severe, but when he was with her he mellowed.

Soon, Clarice and Colley's meetings about her work were held behind closed doors in her studio. Shorter's interest developed to the extent that they were clearly more than friends. This was a highly unusual situation in the Potteries at that time. It was unheard of for the owner of a potbank, an upper-class married man with two children, to mix socially with a single girl from a working-class family. Occasionally factory owners had relationships with female staff, but this was generally done discreetly and they would certainly never socialise with them in public. Inevitably, workers at the factory soon assumed that Clarice and Colley were emotionally involved and events in the following years were to confirm this.

The significance of the close relationship between Clarice and Colley must not be underestimated. He was a bright, well-educated man, with a taste for antiques. By 1926 he had moved into a turn of the century *Arts & Crafts* house at Clayton,

This page, opposite and pages 26, 29:

Autumn (Balloon Trees)
Bizarre
1930-1934 (matchings until 1940)
Trees with sinuous trunks by bushes and a small cottage in a wood . Colourways too numerous to classify but major ones named after dominant foliage colour. Most common is blue, the original was red and variations include orange, yellow, green, pastel.
Colourways:
Blue ★★★£££
Red ★★★★£££££
Variations ★★★£££

designed by Parker & Unwin. He was filling it with eighteenth and nineteenth century furniture and pottery - he particularly loved Oriental antiques.

Born in 1882, Colley was seventeen years older than Clarice, and was tall and distinguished. He had a reputation as a ruthless businessman that was well deserved. He did not concur with the establishment in the Potteries, whose committees often issued edicts he disagreed with. Although they tried to snub him at the time, the extreme success he was soon to enjoy with Clarice's innovative ware was an embarrassment to them as it went against their basic principles. Their negativity towards Colley Shorter was later manifested against Clarice Cliff, even today her achievements are not accepted everywhere in the Potteries.

The next significant event occurred in 1927 when Clarice found a use for the large amount of undecorated, poor-quality earthenware that Wilkinson's had inherited when they bought Newport. She suggested that it could be decorated in bright and bold designs to hide its defects. Some of Wilkinson's salesman scoffed at this idea but Colley Shorter liked it. He took Gladys Scarlett, a seventeen year old paintress from the Wilkinson's decorating shop run by Dolly Cliff. Under Clarice's supervision Gladys started to decorate the old Newport ware.

The first designs were simple triangles, mainly outlined in a rusty-red called Harrison's Red, or green. These were then coloured in with blue, orange, brown or yellow. The rest of the piece was banded in these colours, ensuring that this decoration covered the defects in the body and glaze. A source for this seemingly simple style was probably the Egyptian motifs that were popular at the time. Gladys was to exaggerate her brushstrokes to make it obvious the ware was hand-painted, as this was seen as a potential selling point.

The output of this shop was kept secret from the rest of the factory, as Colley Shorter knew only too well how often designs were stolen in the Potteries. Pieces were taken secretly for firing and then returned to Clarice and Colley for inspection. He must have been excited about its sales prospects, as the old shapes it was decorated on had cost him nothing. At this stage, the ware was un-named, the project developed slowly.

Gladys Scarlett recalled that she was left to her own devices when Clarice went away to the Royal College of Art at Kensington in London. Clarice studied, "Modelling the head and figure from life, figure composition and life drawing". This was for two one-month courses between March and May 1927. That Colley Shorter paid for Clarice to attend the college was highly unusual as he was known to be extremely tight with money. He clearly had belief in her potential. The outcome of her studies was recorded in a letter to Colley Shorter by her tutor, Professor Ledward, and showed that at 28 years of age Clarice still had a lot to learn.

"*She has a natural facility as a modeller, but she is inclined to give a superficial finish to her work owing to her lack of knowledge of the construction of the human figure.*"

Whether or not Clarice saw this report we do not know, but we do know that at this time she went for a brief visit to Paris. It is unthinkable that she went alone. We inevitably conclude that the catalyst was an invitation from Colley. He would certainly have been very aware of the growing interest in modern European shapes, and this was an excellent reason to get her to go with him. All we know about the trip is that it was taken very discreetly.

The French influence on her work was a clear reflection of what she saw in Paris. We can conclude that Colley took Clarice to Museums and Galleries during the visit, where she encountered a lot of new material in a short space of time. Her designs between 1929 and 1931 were influenced by an awareness of Cubism and Impressionism; her use of colour was to be as brave as the Fauvists.

We always associate Clarice Cliff with colour, it was in Paris that she came across her biggest influence in this respect. Surprisingly, not a famous or rising painter, but an artist whose work was mainly in the industrial field, and who even now deserves greater recognition. Clarice was inspired by the pochoir prints of Edouard Benedictus. Back in England she purchased two folios of his designs, Variations and Nouvelle Variations, as well as two folios of a lesser known artist Serge Gladky.

Opposite:
Bizarre
1930-1936
Clarice Cliff's first range of geometric designs. Brush outlined diamonds or triangles, generally randomly coloured, and issued only on old Newport Pottery and Wilkinson's ware, before Clarice designed her own shapes. Referred to in later factory literature as *Original Bizarre* : from 1930 onwards was the umbrella range name of all Clarice Cliff ware, until name was discontinued in 1936: prices very variable, depending on colours used, condition paramount.
The Bizarre girls used the name Pyramids in the factory for Original Bizarre.
★★★££ to ££££

Clarice's dynamic use of colour was to be teamed with the ability to create ceramics in shapes others had needed metal to produce. Although some of her shapes can be traced to a particular source, a lot of her work was to have just the feel of the style. Perhaps the fleeting impressions she retained whilst dashing around Paris, were more important than the magazines she subscribed to after her visit?

Though brief, the 1927 trip had a profound effect on her. Having left school at thirteen Clarice must have experienced culture shock. Certainly, her interests and her work changed dramatically after she returned, producing a whole new style of ceramics.

This page:
Autumn (Balloon Trees)
See page 22.

Opposite:
Bird of Paradise
Appliqué
1930
A yellow and red bird on a branch heavy with black berries, against a green hill side.
★★★★★£££££

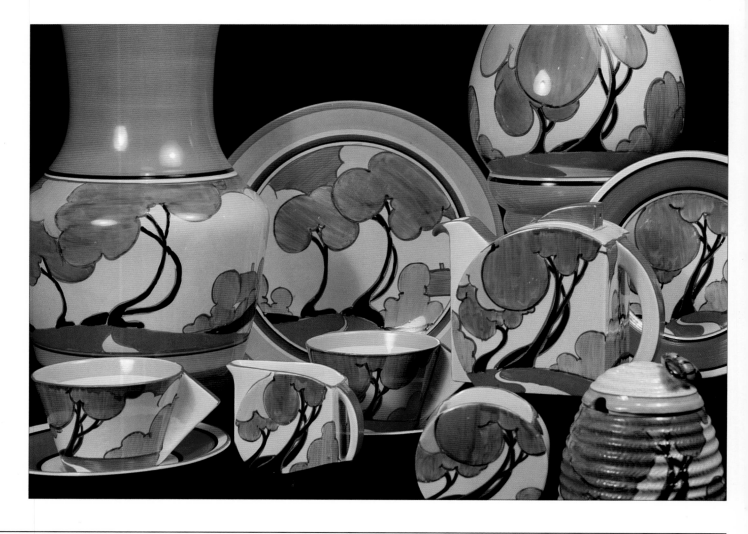

CHAPTER 2

1928

THE BEGINNING OF BIZARRE

Opposite:
Autumn (Balloon Trees)
See page 22.

Bursting with ideas, Clarice intensified the work on the trial pieces in the first few months of 1928. She brought in more paintresses to produce the ware, including Annie Beresford, Mary Brown, Cissy Rhodes, Vera Hollins, Nellie Harrison, Florrie Winkle, Clara Thomas, Phyllis Tharme and Nancy Liversage. At Colley's suggestion, Clarice took most of these girls from her sister Dolly's shop. Dolly's young apprentices were now skilled at hand-painting, and went straight to work for Clarice. At this time the girls were working in a corner of the Newport Pottery showroom and were supervised by George Johnson, but when he left Clarice was given complete charge of them.

A rudimentary production system was established, with some girls outlining, others then enamelling the colours, a bander and liner finishing the ware. Annie Beresford recalled these early days, and how she became an outliner, or "tracer" as she called it.

"I was just mixing paint at first, but after a while I became a tracer and Clarice said she thought I'd do well at this. First of all we had great big ewers (Lotus jugs) as we called them; Clarice would do lines around them and then showed me how to do the diamonds between the lines."

As production grew, Colley Shorter and Clarice Cliff had one of their private meetings in her studio, where Clarice chose the name for the ware. The girls were told to paint it on each piece next to the old Newport Pottery mark it already bore. The word was *Bizarre.*

An article in Pottery Gazette in March 1928 was the very first on *Bizarre*, and shows that the name must have been introduced by February that year at the latest. What the journalist noted on his visit stimulated him to write at length.

"There has recently been established at Newport Pottery a special department which might also be likened to a studio. It consists for the time being of a single room in which is to be found a group of young ladies working under the personal superintendence of a mistress instructor, who, whilst herself creating new freehand styles of decoration, and applying these direct to pieces of ornamental pottery, simultaneously holds a watching brief over what is being done by her apprentices. It is quite a delight to watch this coterie of handcraft decorators - for the most part, we believe, if not entirely, the product of the local art schools - giving free expression to their artistic inclinations direct upon pottery."

Despite its verbose style, this article shows that the production process was established, and it was also the first to name the ware.

"A new range of wares that has been produced under such conditions as we have endeavoured to depict has been styled 'Bizarre Ware', and if the name is intended to convey that the designs are singular and capricious, then it is indeed thoroughly apt."

However, the most amazing thing about the article was the foresight the writer had.

"With the elimination of much of the bric-a-brac that was a heritage of the Victorian era the chances are that ornamental pottery with bold and courageous designs treated in vivacious colourings will more and more experience a vogue. It is possible that the Newport Pottery Co. Ltd. have but succeeded, as yet, in touching the fringe of the field to which the new movement may ultimately lead them."

The writer obviously realised that the process would allow any number of designs to be produced, and would undoubtedly have spoken with Colley Shorter at the factory. It is interesting that Clarice was not mentioned, though she was clearly referred to as the "mistress instructor". Crediting her as the designer as a way of promoting the ware, was yet to happen.

It is hard to appreciate the effect the simple, brashly executed, triangle designs had on the market when launched, but as the writer also observed;

"The majority of women do like, and will have colour, even though it may be simply riotous in its presentation."

The design and production of several other ranges were to take up Clarice's time in March and April before she was able to progress the evolution of *Bizarre* ware. Colley Shorter was aware of the success other potbanks enjoyed with ware featuring child-like motifs designed for children but clearly aimed at adults, he decided to embark on this area of the market.

The story has probably been embellished over the years, but it seems basically true. Apparently Colley saw some drawings done by his youngest daughter Joan featuring "matchstick" people. He took a selection of them into the factory, where he asked Clarice to adapt them. She produced them for plates, bowls, and cups, taking the drawings to her paintresses to execute. This was ironic, as most of them were only six years older than Joan Shorter.

Clarice threw herself into the project. She modelled some original shapes based on nursery rhyme characters. The teapot was *Bones the Butcher*, who wore a butcher's apron; the milk jug was *Boy Blue*, and the sugar called *Humpty* was clearly *Humpty Dumpty*. A *Subway Sadie* comport had *Sadie* as the handle in the middle. She seems to have no connection with nursery rhymes, but has since become the most collectable of the series.

From a Child to a Child, as Colley Shorter called it initially, was launched in May 1928, each piece was marked, *Joan Shorter aged 8*. Colley used Joan in his publicity; she was interviewed for magazines and pictured with the ware. Despite the originality of the modelled teaware, and the publicity it attracted, sales were

disappointing. Several attempts were made to stimulate sales in the following two years, including further designs and more publicity, the caption on the ware became *Joan Shorter aged 9*.

In putting his daughter's name on the ware, Colley may have inadvertently put one of the final pieces into place to launch Clarice: within two months the hand-painted Bizarre mark was replaced with a printed mark: Hand-painted *Bizarre* by Clarice Cliff Newport Pottery England.

The linking of the Bizarre range to a designer proved a major step for Clarice and Colley. Having seen so many signed ceramic and glass pieces during their Paris trip, it was a natural step to use this device to add prestige to the ware. Adding Clarice Cliff's name to the ware gave the factory a personality they could link with the pottery. For the first time, ceramics marketed primarily at women were being designed by a woman.

The other key ingredient needed to complete the formula that launched *Bizarre* was the raw talent to decorate ware. A year previously in July 1927, Colley had been sent a letter by the British Pottery Manufacturer's Association. It offered the services of, "Twenty boys and twenty girls aged 15 to 16 (who) will have completed a two year course and be available for employment in various branches of the Pottery industry from July next." The letter then said, "The twenty girls wish to take up pottery decoration, eight of the boys wish to become pottery designers, two throwers, three modellers and mould makers, and two engravers." This is interesting as it shows that even as late as 1927, the pre-apprenticeship training classes at the Burslem School of Art clearly did not groom young girls as potential designers - not a single one had aspired to this. Conversely, only five of the boys wanted to be decorators, fifteen saw themselves as throwers, modellers, mould makers, or engravers. This puts Clarice's achievement into perspective, not only did she assert herself as a designer, but also was credited for it in an industry that rarely acknowledged the importance of design.

Colley Shorter used this source of partly-trained apprentices both at Wilkinson's and

This page:
Blue Firs
Bizarre
1933-1937
A pen outlined green landscape with blue fir trees, in the foreground a beach and cottage (not on later pieces).
Full scene ★★★£££
Shoulder pattern ★★★££
See also *Coral Firs* and *Green Firs*.

Opposite:
Blue 'W'
Bizarre
1929-1930
The pattern name is taken from the blue 'W' motif around which the design is constructed. It is one of the most complex abstract designs and features a number of interlocking elements consisting of circles, curves and oblong shapes in blue, green, yellow, orange, black and lilac. The execution can vary from a simple version with one or two elements only to a very complex example featuring multiple images of the blue 'W' and other motifs. Equally some versions have no banding whilst others are banded in many colours.
★★★★£££££

Top:
Avon
Clarice Cliff
1936-1937
A pen outline design in pastel colours on a green glaze with a bridge over a river and two fisherman.

★★★★★££

Opposite:
Bridgwater
Bizarre
1934
A pen outline design of a question-mark shape tree by a river with reeds, with a bridge and cottage in background. A few examples are known where the bridge and roof are blue, this is classified as *Bridgwater Blue*.

Colourways:
Orange ★★★★££££
Green ★★★£££
Blue ★★★★★££££

Bottom:
Peter Pan Crocus
Bizarre
1930-1932
Hand-painted *Autumn Crocus* flowers against a black print of a tree in silhouette with small rabbits under it.
Referred to as Awakening in factory literature.

★★★££

Newport. In July 1928 John Shaw, Harold Walker, Tom Stringer, Ellen Browne and Nellie Webb joined the embryonic Bizarre shop, later those at Wilkinson's were also to be transferred. These talented decorators needed little training and the output of Bizarre increased dramatically.

Colley Shorter was now able to intensify the marketing of Bizarre, giving the job to his top salesman Ewart Oakes. He was a, "Sturdy, well built man, very congenial to everybody", and a strong supporter of Port Vale Football Club. Ewart had joined Wilkinson's originally in 1914, by 1919 he had established a strong liaison with his customers, covering all the South of England except the London area. His response on seeing the ware was sceptical, but aware of Colley's belief in its potential, and knowing Clarice quite well, he played along whilst believing it would not sell.

Ewart Oakes did not drive, but because of the importance of this venture Colley Shorter sent him in his own car driven by the chauffeur Herbert Webb. His first call was at William Baker & Son of Oxford. Their China and Glass department had a lady buyer and Ewart recalled she was "agog" at the sight of Bizarre - and bought the carload on the spot!

Ironically, after his initial doubts Ewart was instrumental in the success of Bizarre as he secured many more orders than the various salesmen who covered the north-east and north-west. His reward for selling so much, in what started out as a depressed market, was a commission of one and a quarter percent of sales; this was a considerable amount between 1928 and 1939. The fact that Mr. Colley was always behind with these payments, was a key reason why Ewart stayed with the company.

The chauffeur Herbert Webb got to know Clarice at this time, his memories give an interesting insight into how quickly her life was changing. He had been told to give Clarice lifts whenever it was convenient, shortly after this she paid him £5 to teach her to drive. In 1928 there was no test, and as soon as Clarice felt confident she went with Herbert to Holland & Hollinshead an Austin dealership, in Alsager. There, she bought herself a car. It was an Austin Seven, for which she paid £60, a fortune compared to the six shillings a week her paintresses were earning at the time. In her usual Bizarre manner she named the car "Jenny", and she was now able to drive herself to work. Naturally this raised quite a few eyebrows amongst the factory staff.

Having already given Clarice the chance to produce some extremely adventurous ware, and set up the special hand-painting shop at Newport, Colley Shorter's next move was to further embellish the reputation of Clarice and Bizarre. Using publicity in a way that kept him ahead of his competitors, in August 1928 he arranged to launch the ware at Waring & Gillow's store in London. This was more than just a display of Bizarre, he arranged for some of the paintresses to do a painting demonstration. In the foyer of the store, an area was set up where Gladys Scarlett outlined and enamelled, and Nellie Harrison and Florrie Winkle banded. Although she was shown decorating pieces in the demonstration photograph, Clarice was already more than just a paintress. She painted briefly for the picture, then spent the rest of the time with Colley Shorter who only visited the exhibition for a couple of hours each day. This further fuelled the speculation about their friendship in the factory. By September the designs had progressed from the simple triangles of early 1928. More complex geometric and linear designs were appearing. However, Clarice's designs were mainly still limited to old Newport and Wilkinson's shapes. These included a vase shape 120, an Athens shape jug and beakers lemonade set, and more old-fashioned Newport Pottery jugs and bowls.

Around this time Clarice introduced what was to become her best-selling design. Her inspiration was some hand-painted pieces done a few years earlier by John Butler, which had large white and purple Crocus flowers on highly glazed ware. Her idea was to produce clusters of the flowers, in orange, blue and purple. Her Crocus seems simple but it is really very clever. The petals were realistically created with a few skillful flicks of the brush down the ware, then by turning the ware upside down the thin green leaves were applied equally speedily. One of the most subtle things about Crocus was explained by Clarice to one of her paintresses; the brown banding below represents the earth, the yellow above, the sun.

The first girl to do Crocus was Ethel Barrow, a confident and out-going Wilkinson's

Bottom left:
Acorn
Bizarre
1934
Pen outline of red acorns with green and brown oak leaves against tan and yellow runnings.
★★★££

Bottom right:
Amberose
Bizarre
1933-1934
Red and yellow roses, with green foliage. Generally found on Daffodil shape tableware.
★★★★£££

Top:
Brookfields
Bizarre and Clarice Cliff
1936
A pen outline in yellow of a cottage and garage, next to a bridge and ploughed field in brown, green and yellow, the whole design covered with fine blue and yellow lines, which are omitted on awkward shapes.
★★£££

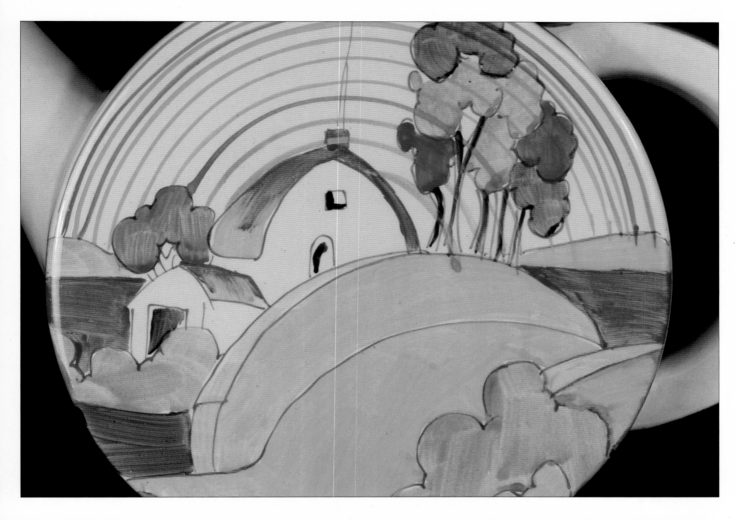

paintress. Clarice showed her the design as she had painted it as a water-colour, and asked her to execute it on a cup and saucer. Clarice was pleased how she did it, and Ethel moved across to Newport and became the *Crocus* Girl. Originally, Ethel did all the flowers, Nellie Webb or Winnie Pound the leaves, and Clara Thomas the banding. *Crocus* was so successful, however, that Ethel's job was then enlarged to training teams of girls to do it.

Throughout the Thirties *Crocus* continued to be produced on nearly every shape the factory issued and in various colourways, making it Clarice's signature design. It sold well not just for the *Bizarre* years, but right through until 1963.

By September 1928 the factory was so busy that there was a shortage of paintresses, so Clarice advertised in the Stoke-on-Trent Evening Sentinel. "Girls wanted to learn freehand painting. Apply Miss Clarice Cliff Newport Pottery". One girl who responded to this was 14-year-old Marjory Higginson, who vividly recalled the interview:

"*I carried a folio of my school artwork to Newport Pottery where I was seen by Clarice Cliff herself. I remember her now in a blue georgette dress, she was very smart. She wore high heels because she was very small, and had her black hair pulled back in a bun. I thought that Clarice was only 22 at this time and was surprised to find she was 29. I was terribly disappointed because she told me she didn't need anyone as she had taken someone on that morning. But I showed her some of my paintings and she said, 'Well in your case we'll take you on as you are already interested in painting.' I started on the Monday morning at five shillings and seven pence a week.*"

It was left to Gladys Scarlett to show these new girls how to execute *Bizarre*. Gladys was a slim, blue-eyed blonde who the girls remember as being proud of her appearance. One of her favourite colours was pink and as she made her own clothes, her enthusiasm to show these new outfits meant she often arrived at work wearing pink dresses. On one occasion her lack of ability as a seamstress meant that she had

This page:
Bamboo
Bizarre
1935 (matchings to 1939)
An etched design of a brown and orange oriental cottage, with bamboo with green leaves and yellow *Rhodanthe* style flowers.
★★★£

Opposite:
Broth
Fantasque
1929-1931
Shapes resembling the cooled fat on top of broth. This was an adaptation of a John Butler design produced at Wilkinson's when Clarice was training. It was firstly numbered Fantasque 105, then named.
Colourways:
Orange ★★★£££
Red ★★★★£££

Top:
Beach Ball
Bizarre
1932
Two segmented black and orange balls with leaves each side surrounded by narrow green and orange vertrical panels.
★★★★★£££

Bottom:
Bermuda
Clarice Cliff
1936-1937
A pen outline design with gnarled tree with a blue, brown and red trunk, blue and yellow foliage, on a green/ brown ground.
★★★★£

Opposite:
Cafe-au-Lait
1931-1934
A process of decorating by using a special brush to apply stippled colour on all or part of the ware, which was then painted in a design. Examples include *Red Roofs, Bobbins, Berries, Trees & House, Summerhouse* and *Autumn.* Also used to decorate ware, which had a small simple floral or fruit motif added.

The technique was also used for parts of the May Avenue, Japan and Trallee designs.
See also *Nuage.*

to hold her creation together with pins until she went home. The girls noticed that Clarice disapproved of Gladys, whom Colley called his "little girl in pink". Sometimes he took flowers in for Clarice, and occasionally for Gladys. If he stopped at her bench to have a chat it did not go down well with Clarice. This perhaps further indicates that Clarice was already emotionally involved with Colley Shorter.

The new girls joining Clarice meant she now had twenty-five decorators. All these girls were just 14 or 15 years of age, the factory workers initially called them the *Bizarre* babes. As they matured they were soon collectively referred to as the *Bizarre* girls. Had Clarice used mature paintresses they would have executed her designs too regularly to have any character; the beauty of *Bizarre* was the teams of nimble young minds and fingers, with no artistic pre-conceptions, giving it a charming naiveté.

To create a production-line for *Bizarre* an area of a building next to the canal at Newport Pottery was adapted by the factory workmen into a proper shop. Wooden benches each seating four of Clarice's decorators ran the length of the room. On the opposite wall were stillages to hold the ware as it went through the decorating process, from here it was carried to the two enamel kilns on the Newport site.

Around this time, Clarice had to assert herself over some of the older workers who treated her as an equal. Under Colley Shorter's influence her confidence had grown, and probably at his suggestion she established her authority. The catalyst for this came about when a warehouse-woman asked her, "What should I do with this, Clarice?". She answered sternly, "Don't you think it's time you started to call me Miss Cliff?". The *Bizarre* girls knew that she treated them specially, being protective of her decorating shop, but even they had to refer to her as "Miss Cliff".

Running the large decorating shop became a full time job, so Clarice put a former Wilkinson's paintress Lily Slater in charge as the missus. An insight into Clarice's personality at this time is given by Annie Beresford.

"*Miss Cliff used to sit with us and help us but never seemed over enthusiastic about*

This page:
Bignou
Bizarre
1930
A sunburst in green, orange and yellow, a shoulder pattern on tea and dinner ware.
★★★££

Opposite:
Canterbury Bells
Bizarre
1932-1933
Freehand blue, orange and yellow flowers, with a Cafe-au-Lait ground, brown above and yellow below.
This is often confused with Solomon's Seal.
★★£££
See also *Petunia*.

Opposite:
Petunia
Bizarre
1933
Freehand flowers, strangely not Petunia flowers, but the name given to the alternate colourway of *Canterbury Bells*.
★★★★£££
See also *Canterbury Bells*.

what we were doing. To me she was quite a sedate sort of person, and we thought the world of her. A memory comes to me of Armistice Day. Miss Cliff made us stop working so we could honour the two minute silence. I don't know whether she had lost anyone in the 1914 - 1918 War, but she looked very sad. "

Freed from the day to day responsibility of running the *Bizarre* shop, Clarice only really came into contact with her outliners when she would take them her water-colour drawings of new designs, so sample pieces could be made. Clarice now had more time to model and design; this led to an even greater burst of productivity than she had achieved in 1928.

This page:
Age of Jazz figures
1930
These figures are from a series of five produced in 1930. Illustrated are shape 436 the pianist, shape 435 the drummer and shape 434 two dancing couples.
★★★★★£££££

Opposite:
Caravan
Appliqué
1930
A caravan on a hillside, under a tree heavy with oranges.
★★★★★£££££

CHAPTER 3

1929

NEW SHAPES AND GLAZES

"*Newport Pottery was just one building in the middle of a site which looked as if they dropped a bomb on it! Wilkinson's was an active firm with printing shops and offices and you went through their part of the site and passed a number of empty derelict buildings, like a wilderness, to get to Newport. The only thing with any life in it was the Newport Pottery block. You did not feel like part of a large firm, it was very individual.*"

These memories of paintress May Keeling vividly bring to life what is was like for the girls who worked for Clarice in 1929. However, although the *Bizarre* shop was uppermost in her mind, at the time Newport Pottery did have its own mould-makers, flatware and casting shops and sliphouse, plus the necessary joinery and maintenance staff to keep the site running. As sales of *Bizarre* increased, so more of the shops were utilised for various processes.

In the administrative offices at Newport, the youngest recruit was Stan Critchlow, the office boy. His job was to answer the telephone and look after the post, so he was always in contact with Clarice and Colley. He remembers Mr. Colley as being very severe, but Clarice had a soft spot for him. He was small, and went to work in short trousers, Clarice would chat with him when she went into the office. He remembered Clarice peering into a kaleidoscope, which he supposed she used to inspire some of her early designs. One day she asked him to stand against the wall, she marked his height and the date on it in pencil. This was to be repeated with Clarice saying to Stan "Let's see if you have grown!"

Opposite:
Arabesque
Bizarre
1929-1930
An Isnic style design in red, green, blue and yellow, probably only produced as a sample.
★★★★★£££

This page:
Blossom
Appliqué and Latona
1930
Freehand clematis and lilac flowers in purple and red, against a trellis.
Latona: ★★★★★£££
Appliqué: ★★★★★££££

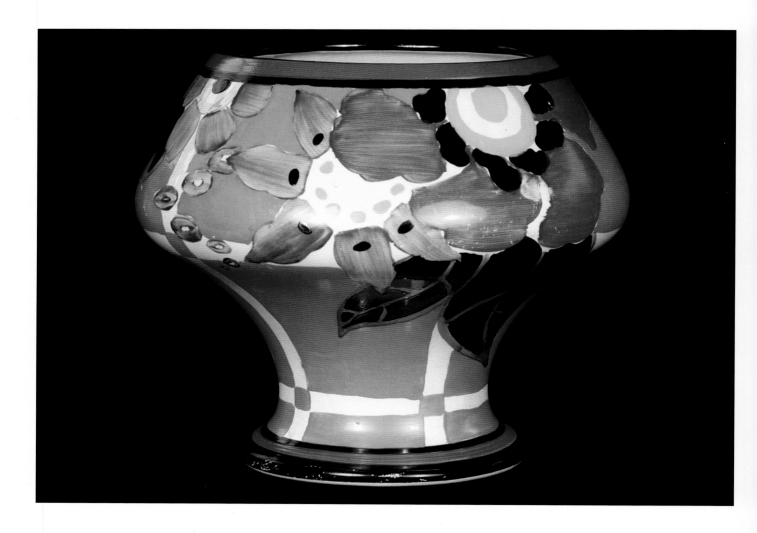

Whilst 1928 was the year Clarice Cliff made her mark with *Bizarre* and then *Crocus*, 1929 was dominated by her production of new shapes and glazes. In quick succession the *Inspiration* and *Latona* glazes were launched. Using squares, circles and cones in her uniquely artistic way, Clarice then produced over fifty new shapes. The launch of her *Fantasque* designs - from June onwards - finally established her as an innovator of ceramic designs.

With the supply of old Newport shapes depleted, Clarice embraced the chance to produce new shapes during this year. To appreciate the changes Clarice introduced it is necessary to understand the numbering system. Shapes in production were given shape numbers for ordering purposes, pre-1929 ones were in the sequence up to 342. However, these numbers were not always issued chronologically, some had never been used, others had been issued and withdrawn as they did not sell. Shape numbers before 342 date from between 1919 and 1928, although Clarice was only really responsible for originating the later shapes up to 1928.

Some popular shapes were classified by names, although these were in the minority. The *Lotus* jug that was to be produced in great quantities in *Bizarre* designs had originally been designed as the water jug of a seven piece toilet set in 1919. With the change to it being sold as a decorative flower jug, the factory also re-classified it as an *Isis* jug in 1930. However, with thousands of examples produced with *Lotus* shape impressed in the base, collectors retain its original name, using *Isis* for the same shape without handles.

Since origination and production of new shapes was expensive the factory avoided doing it unless necessary, as it already had what it saw as a perfectly functional range of vases, bowls, jardinieres, fancies, tea and coffee ware. Naturally with her new ideas Clarice thought these old fashioned and not the ideal shape for her designs. The factory already had large jardinieres in the conservative *Bowness* and *Chippendale* shapes. However, Clarice created a more streamlined shape, which she called *Dover*. This was to remain in production throughout the Thirties, long after the other shapes had been discontinued.

This page:
Blue Daisy
Bizarre
1930
A stylised orange, blue and purple daisy painted freehand, with blue and purple banded and striped pattern either side.
★★★★★££

Opposite:
Carpet
Bizarre
1930-1931
Curvilinear shapes, stripes and dots, in coral red or orange with grey and black, based on a carpet design by Da Silva Bruhns. Colourways orange and red.
★★★★£££££

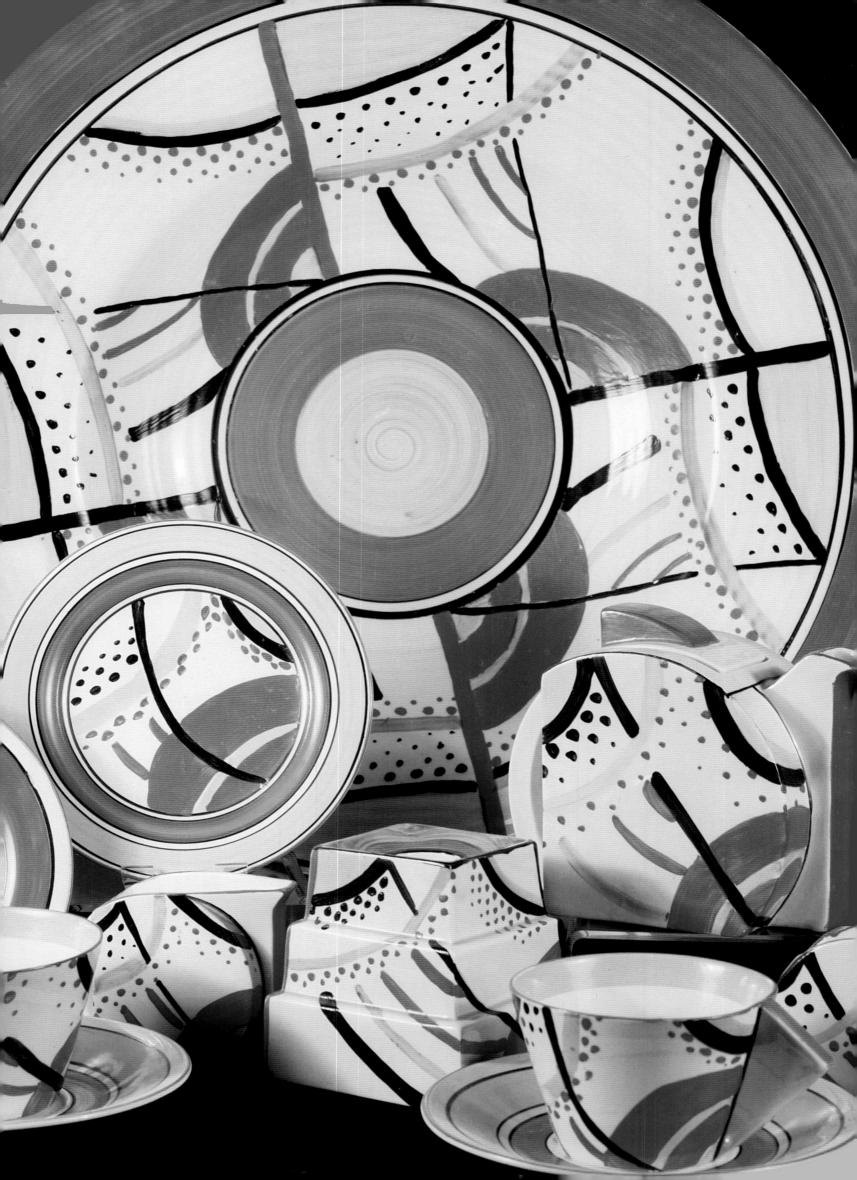

At the beginning of 1929 Clarice was finally in a position to make decisions about the shapes the factory issued, as witnessed by the mass of new shapes which appeared in just a few months. Reviewing the extant shape sheets, it is possible to trace her influence from around shape 341 onwards, she was certainly responsible for the smooth clean shapes 358 and 360. The on-glaze style of hand-painting was easier to execute on ware with a regular surface, these shapes were perfect for it, particularly the banding that united the central design to the shape.

Clarice made a series of round or square tiered bowls and vases early in 1929. She was influenced by the geometrically-shaped ware of the French designer Robert Lallemant she had seen in the magazine *Mobilier et Décoration*. However, each of her shapes was an original, for which Lallemant's pieces suggested an idea not an end product.

The geometrically shaped pieces in the sequence 366 to 369 were intended to be complementary to her geometric designs. They were based on the circle or the square and had no surface ornamentation or fussy handles. No one else in the Potteries was producing such shapes at the time. Appearing early in 1929, they represent Clarice's earliest Art Deco work.

Until now the significance of the shapes 366 to 369 has been overlooked. Clarice's tiered vases pre-date pieces that Keith Murray produced for Wedgwood from 1932 onwards, which achieved a similar clean geometric feel with heavy grooves around the ware. At the time they were first issued shapes 366 to 369 were made in very limited quantities and were over-shadowed by the vast *Conical* range that followed within weeks. Had the shapes been produced in greater quantity when issued, they might have provided the core of Clarice Cliff's output in 1929, but they were over-looked in what was one of her busiest years. This is why most examples of these pivotal shapes are confusingly in designs issued between 1930 and 1935. Clarice's landscapes had to traverse each of the tiered layers, for which the shapes were not really suited but this gave a *Bizarre* combination of shape and design.

Opposite:
**Castellated Circle
(Green Circle)**
Bizarre
1929-1930
Abstract design of circular and castellated shapes, some with solid colour, sometimes with triangles behind. Confusingly variously coloured, the circles are mostly solid black, black and yellow or green and orange.
★★★★££££

This page:
This picture shows Clarice's first geometric shapes.
Top row, left to right:
Shape 360, shape 369, shape 392, shape 391 and shape 358.
Bottom row, left to right:
Shape 365, shape 366, shape 368 and shape 362.

Clarice demonstrated a further quality at this time, that one might call ceramic lateral thinking. These new geometrically-shaped vases followed formal lines, by inverting them she created further shapes. The inverted 369, slimmed down, made the candlestick shape 392, the square tiered *Fernpot* 368, became candlestick shape 391. Her most successful "inversions" were of the vase shapes 358 and 360, which upside down became vases 362 and 365 respectively. One vase we know Clarice did copy from *Mobilier et Décoration* was the next one in the number sequence, a shape 370. This was a simple globe with an aperture at the top. These early 1929 shapes were to become mainstays of her output throughout the *Bizarre* years.

In the Clarice Cliff archives of 1929 is a watercolour design of a fantastic landscape with brash trees in blue, green and orange, and a bridge that looks like something out of a Disney cartoon. The design represents somewhat of a puzzle. We find it on bowls and vases which have a large *Bizarre* mark with the design name *Caprice*, hand painted above. Every example of *Caprice* is on a grey matt glaze, not used on any other ware at this time. It pre-dates *Luxor* and *Sunray* which came later in 1929, so it represents Clarice's first full landscape. It was used as the landscape design of the *Inspiration* range later in 1929. The bubble and wedge trees of *Trees & House* were clearly based on those on *Caprice* and it represents the first of the landscapes that were to prove such a key part of Clarice's output from 1930 onwards.

One of the qualities that was to make Clarice's ware so attractive was resolved in 1929. Previously all the ware had been glazed in a solution of two percent iron oxide. This caused the dark runnings in the glaze which gave the ware a heavy look. After experiments, this was reduced to one percent. It was called honeyglaze and this descriptive name described the slightly warm honey colour it gave to the white clay body. It proved to be the ideal background for her bright colours.

Having made her stunning 366 to 369 shapes, it is then puzzling that in the following few months Clarice issued the *Archaic* range as part of *Bizarre*. They were modelled as ornamental columns produced to take classical designs, based on illustrations done

This page:
Blue-Eyed Marigolds
Bizarre
1930
Outlined orange flowers with blue centres, honeyglaze leaves, and a black ground.
★★★★£££

Opposite:
Chintz
Bizarre
1932-1933
Water lily buds and leaves, forming a fabric-like design. Also used as a motif on pattern 5957 in dominant yellow.
Colourways:
Blue or Orange ★★★★£££
Green ★★★★★££££

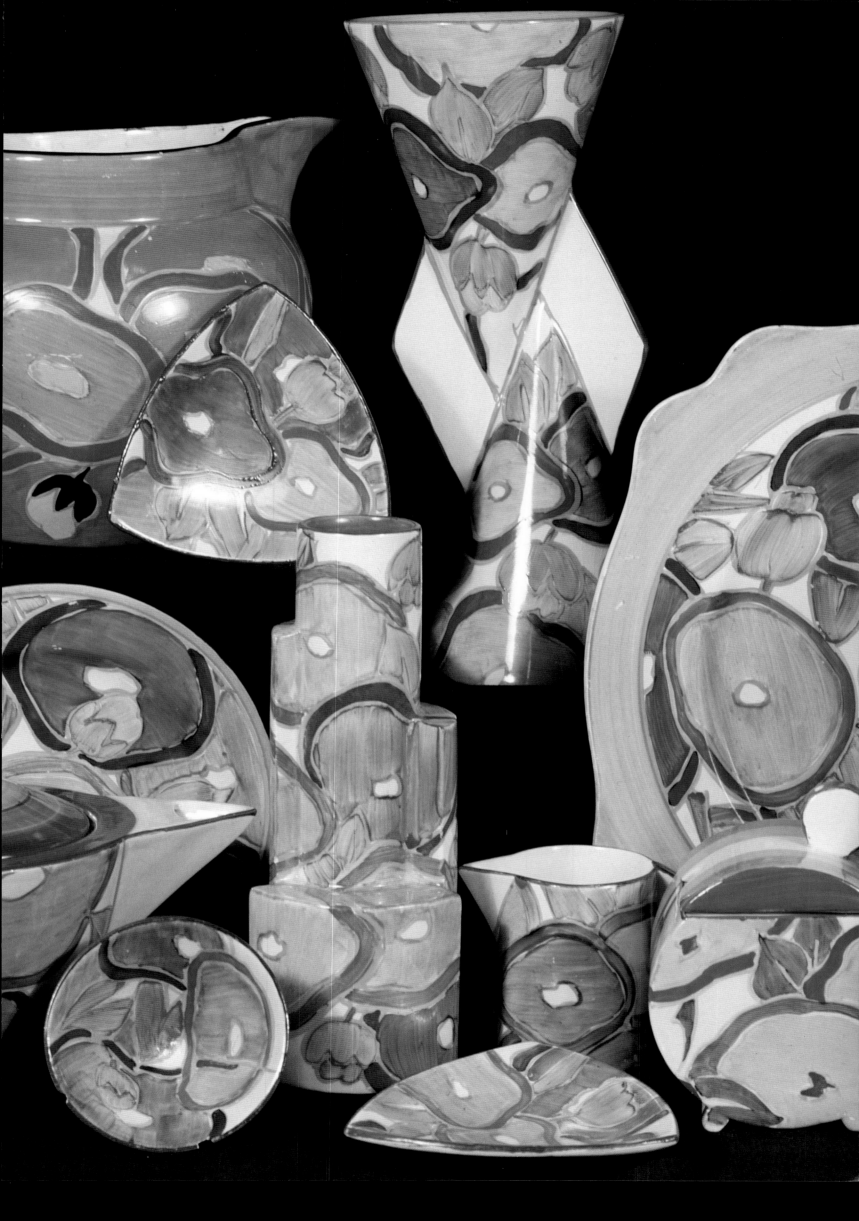

in 1856 by Owen Jones in *"Grammar of Ornament"*. Why did she jump from futuristic shapes to ones that were so traditional? The answer is that these were undoubtedly the idea of Colley Shorter. Well aware of the craze at the time for anything Egyptian, many potteries were producing related ware.

The evolution of the *Archaic* range was known to be one he pioneered, but he obviously needed the services of his most inventive designer. Clarice probably supervised an experienced modeller making the shapes of the *Archaic* vases, which were in the sequence 372 to 377. Each had a modelled top to take the design on the capital of the columns. The source of each design was explained in a printed backstamp on the base, for example, "Replica. The Memnonium, Thebes. Capital of smaller columns 1200 B.C."

Although each piece of the *Archaic* range had the name written in paint, and a *Bizarre* by *Clarice Cliff* mark, further evidence of the genesis of this range is provided by the wording in the advertisements used to launch the ware. Beneath a heading "Nothing new under the sun", these were written in a style typical of Mr. Colley.

"Realising how near to the original principle of art the designs of Bizarre ware really are we have dipped into archaeology to find that the ancients had in their day almost identical styles. We have produced a range of ancient pillar heads both in form and colour."

If Colley Shorter saw some artistic connection between these pieces and *Bizarre*, his customers did not. Despite extensive marketing this ware was a notable failure. Anticipating big sales he had gone ahead with production of many glazed but undecorated stock of the six *Archaic* range shapes. Ironically, within months these were to be issued in a mass of startling new designs in the *Fantasque* and *Appliqué* ranges that were still a twinkle in Clarice Cliff's artistic eye.

At the same time as *Archaic* was being created, Clarice was experimenting in new glazes. These were supervised by Austin Walker, Jack Walker's son, who was the

This page:
Blue Heaven
Bizarre
1930
Known from one example, this could be a sample piece. All painted in blue to give the impression of a stencil, shows a single tree with spear shaped leafs and flowers in a landscape. The pattern was used in *Inspiration* glaze and later in the *Opalesque* range number 6415.
★★★★★£££

Opposite:
Circle Tree (RAF Tree)
Fantasque
1929-1930
A freehand spiky black tree with rainbow-coloured circles.
★★★★£££request

works manager for Newport Pottery. The memories of his young assistant Jim Hall explain how *Inspiration* and then *Latona* were created. Austin Walker knew a Mr. Wildig, a glaze chemist for Malkin's Tile Works, which occupied a small corner site between the pottery and Newport Lane. Jim recalled that during a conversation about soft glazes for tiles, Mr. Wildig suggested using a tile glaze fired to only 760°centigrade instead of the usual 1050°, which gave the ware a soft white absorbent coating. On this Clarice supervised the painting of oxides of copper in a watery state to get a variegated green over the ware. Various types of oxide were used including copper sulphate, and this spread, giving the halo effect to the background decoration. This was what made *Inspiration* unique, as the design was actually in the glaze. Clarice then devised designs to go on this copper background, and these were painted in manganese solutions and iron, and it was then fired again at the normal 1050°centigrade.

In choosing designs to be executed in the *Inspiration* glaze Clarice again excelled. *Caprice* the fantastic landscape produced earlier in the year was executed in blue, purple, lilac, and black against the swirling copper coloured ground, as were various designs with stylised flowers.

Colley Shorter's contribution was again in launching this ware, and his press-release was inspired:

"*Inspiration has created tremendous interest unveiling the secret (which was lost for centuries) of reproducing in a superb matt glaze that gorgeous colour peculiar to Ancient Egyptian Pottery, known as the Scarab Blue. This colour was inspired by the Scarab Beetle, the Egyptian sacred symbol of immortality.*"

In 1929 and 1930 *Inspiration* was the most prestigious line produced for *Bizarre*. However, it proved difficult to produce economically, as the watery glazes meant many pieces were faulty, or damaged by sticking to kiln furniture during firing. There was too high a loss rate to make it a sales success. Whereas a *Bizarre* Lotus jug was

This page:
Bobbins
Bizarre
1931-1933
Blue and green leaves with red and yellow bobbins, often on a *Cafe-au-Lait* ground.
★★★★££££

Opposite:
Comets
Bizarre
1929-1930
Interwoven comet shapes with small floral motifs at their heads.
★★★★££££

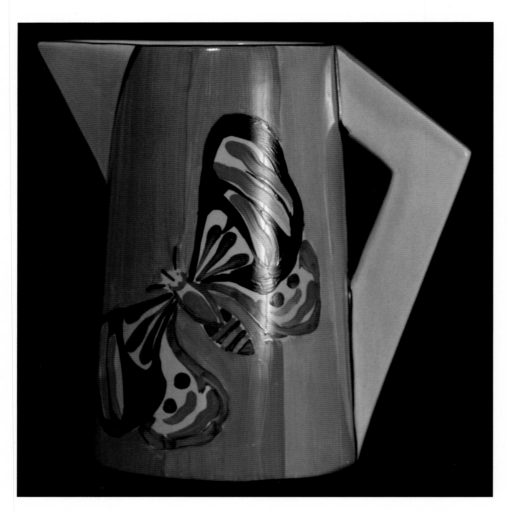

Top:
Butterfly
Bizarre
1929-1930
Colourful freehand butterflies against a striped ground, this was copied from a pochoir print by Edouard Benedictus.
★★★★££

Bottom left:
Blueberry Tree
Bizarre
1933
Styised leafy tree with green and yellow foliage and blue berries. Usually found on *Daffodil* teaware.
★★★★££

Bottom right:
Blue Ribbon
Bizarre
1932
A freehand floral design with orange flowers against a background of blue, green and yellow "ribbons". Red variation known.
★★★★£££

Opposite:
Coral Firs
Bizarre and Tableware
1933-1939
A black pen outline landscape with coral and brown fir trees, a black-roofed cottage and cliffs. The design was simplified to a shoulder pattern on *Biarritz* tableware.
★★£££
See also *Blue Firs* and *Green Firs*.

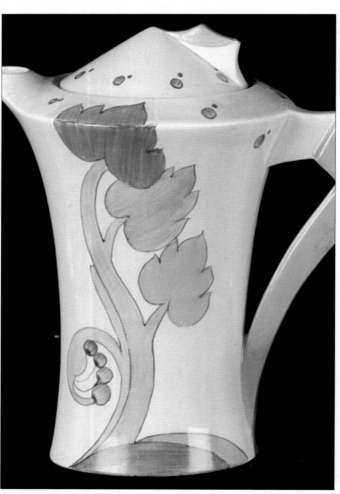

seven shillings and sixpence, an *Inspiration* one was fifteen shillings, or almost three week's wages for a *Bizarre* girl. Ever economical Mr. Colley arranged that rather than being dumped on the shard ruck, the faulty *Inspiration* ware be broken into small pieces, taken to Chetwynd House where it was set into a new concrete path in the garden.

Other new glazes resulted from the experiments that led to *Inspiration*; *Latona* offered customers ware with a milk white glaze. The impact of its launch, a few months after *Inspiration*, was achieved by some new shapes Clarice was designing.

Whilst the *Inspiration* then *Latona* glazes were being pioneered, Clarice went straight from work on the doomed *Archaic* series to another range stylistically centuries away from it. Shapes 378 to 383 follow on from the *Archaic* series numbers, and were the initial pieces in what was to be a pivotal shape in the progression of *Bizarre*. Clarice moved from squares and circles to produce ware based on a cone.

In her *Conical* series, Clarice was finally able to vent all the ideas that had been building up in her, and we know that she made the initial bowls and vases very quickly. The basic idea was of a simple cone, inspired by some goblets produced by French silversmith Desny a few years previously. However, Clarice elaborated greatly on this idea, and the original version, a cone with a round foot (shape 378) a stage further, put an inverted cone underneath it as the base, making her famous *Yo Yo* vase (shape 379). This was adapted as a broader cone resting on a round foot (shape 381), two cones one within the other, resting on a round foot (shape 380). Almost as soon as these were made she adapted the shape into an even purer cone form, by putting four triangular feet under the cone, making her famous *Conical* bowl.

"That bloody woman!" Is the way Bill Lunt the clay manager at Newport referred to Clarice. He was responsible for evolving the *Conical* shapes, and believed these were impossible to produce; he felt sure some of them would not withstand the firing because of their construction. He was proven right over the *Conical* bowl, as initially Clarice insisted its four triangular feet went to the edge of the rim. This caused it to warp when fired, so she relented and it was made with the feet just half way up the sides. Whatever shapes made it to production, we need to be grateful for Clarice's determination; it may not have made her Bill Lunt's favourite person, but in creating the *Conical* range she dramatically changed the mould-makers ideas.

Latona appeared in June 1929, the beauty of the glaze was its matt milky surface. At the same time the early *Conical* pieces were finalised, their selling point was their shape. The two were initially combined and decorated with just simple edge designs of small delicate triangles in orange and black. This combination shows that Clarice found beauty in simplicity.

Judging by the present day rarity, it seems that almost immediately the simple design was dropped and the *Latona* ware was primarily issued in a mass of all-over floral designs painted freehand. Cissy Rhodes believed that she was the only girl to do the tree on *Latona Tree* and also remembers that *Latona Red Roses* was difficult as the red had to be put on so thickly. The new *Latona* range appeared from August onwards, the glaze was then used on many of Clarice Cliff's shapes throughout 1930 and into 1931. However, it was the *Conical* range that was to prove an even bigger success. The futuristic bowl became very fashionable and stockists such as Lawley's ordered thousands of them.

The impetus Clarice's designs and shapes gave the factory by this time was sensational. More decorators had to be employed to keep up with demand; Nancy Lawton and Sadie Maskrey were taken from Wilkinson's, Elsie Nixon and Winnie Pound joined straight from school, the fourth and final boy outliner Fred Salmon, joined from the Newcastle-under-Lyme School of Art.

During June another major part of the Clarice Cliff legend galloped onto the scene. The *Bizooka*, a horse made entirely of *Bizarre* pottery is first recorded in an advertisement dated 1st July 1929. At this time it was just an imaginative drawing of a pottery horse. The eye-catching image began to appear in the adverts for Clarice's ware, and for a while served as a logo for *Bizarre*. It was to become a ceramic reality a few years later.

Opposite:
Cowslip
Bizarre
1933-1934
Stylised leaves in a mottled *Cafe-au-Lait* style ground, in colourways of blue, yellow, green and brown.
★★★★£££

In June 1929 Clarice issued the first new design range to complement *Bizarre*. The evidence of a few early examples indicates it may have originally been called *Fantasy* but from this came her *Fantasque* range.

This served a dual purpose; some retailers were requesting exclusive designs, and sales had grown so quickly that Colley Shorter wanted this ware credited to Wilkinson's rather than Newport to spread the tax bill.

Designs in the *Fantasque* range were originally given numbers, but were so successful that they were then named. The earliest were *Tree*, *Cherry* (102), *Broth* (103), *Lily Orange* (104), *Pebbles* (106), *Lily Brown* (107) and *Kandina*. All these designs were quite broadly executed and experimental as there was no common theme. *Pebbles* and *Cherry* were outlined, whereas *Kandina* was freehand. Only *Broth* and *Lily* were to be produced in any quantity. *Broth* was in fact based on an existing John Butler design.

The success of the *Conical* range led Clarice to develop further shapes for it. Most importantly she created her first teapot. Her original and eye-catching shape was inspired by taking the triangular feet of the *Conical* bowl for the solid handle and a triangular spout. The sugar bowl was a miniature version of the *Conical* bowl, the tiny milk jug also had the same feet, and even the cups were given solid triangular handles. The ideas for these shapes were Clarice's and were a natural progression from the *Conical* ones she had already produced.

The *Conical* teapot was initially issued as part of what the factory called an *Early Morning set*. Subsequently collectors have mistakenly called these "tea for two" sets, which is understandable as they had just two cups and saucers, a milk jug, a sugar bowl and a plate. However, the sets were actually intended for a couple to have tea and piece of toast in bed before getting up, hence the name.

The *Conical* teaware shape caused a sensation when it was launched. Despite criticism from conservative customers about the impracticality of the solid handles, the shape attracted young buyers. The factory found it hard to keep up with demand, although

Opposite:

Café (Cubes)
Bizarre
1932-1933
A panel design of grey and black squares and oblong shapes with either red or orange as an additional colour. A black panel with red or orange dots is also incorporated. On a vase or bowl the design repeats and wraps around.
This design is probably based on the 1928 wall and ceiling designs by Sophie Taeuber-Arp for the very modern Café Aubette in Strasbourg. This tea room designed in collaboration with Theo van Doesburg (see Cubist) was very controversial and even 10 years later was considered by many to be too avante garde. In 1938 new owners completely redecorated it.

★★★★★£££££

This page:

Capri
Bizarre
1935
A garden with bushes and trees, covered in fine bands.
Colourways; green and orange.

★★££

Top:
Caprice
Fantasque
1929
A landscape with fantastic stylised trees and an elaborate bridge. First produced as an on glaze decoration on a grey glaze. Also used for the *Inspiration* series.

★★★★£££

See also *Inspiration Caprice*.

Bottom:
Celtic Harvest
Clarice Cliff
1937-1941 and post war
A range with surface ornamentation of corn sheaves and fruit, with handpainted coloured detail, produced on a very large range of tableware and fancies, with a number of glaze variations.

★£

See also page 223.

Opposite:
Crayon Scenes
Bizarre
1934
Produced using ceramic crayons, a set of at least twelve sketched landscapes drawn freehand in natural colours, featuring very English scenes with churches, trees, and bridges, some were named.
All examples decorated by paintress Rene Dale.

★★★★£££

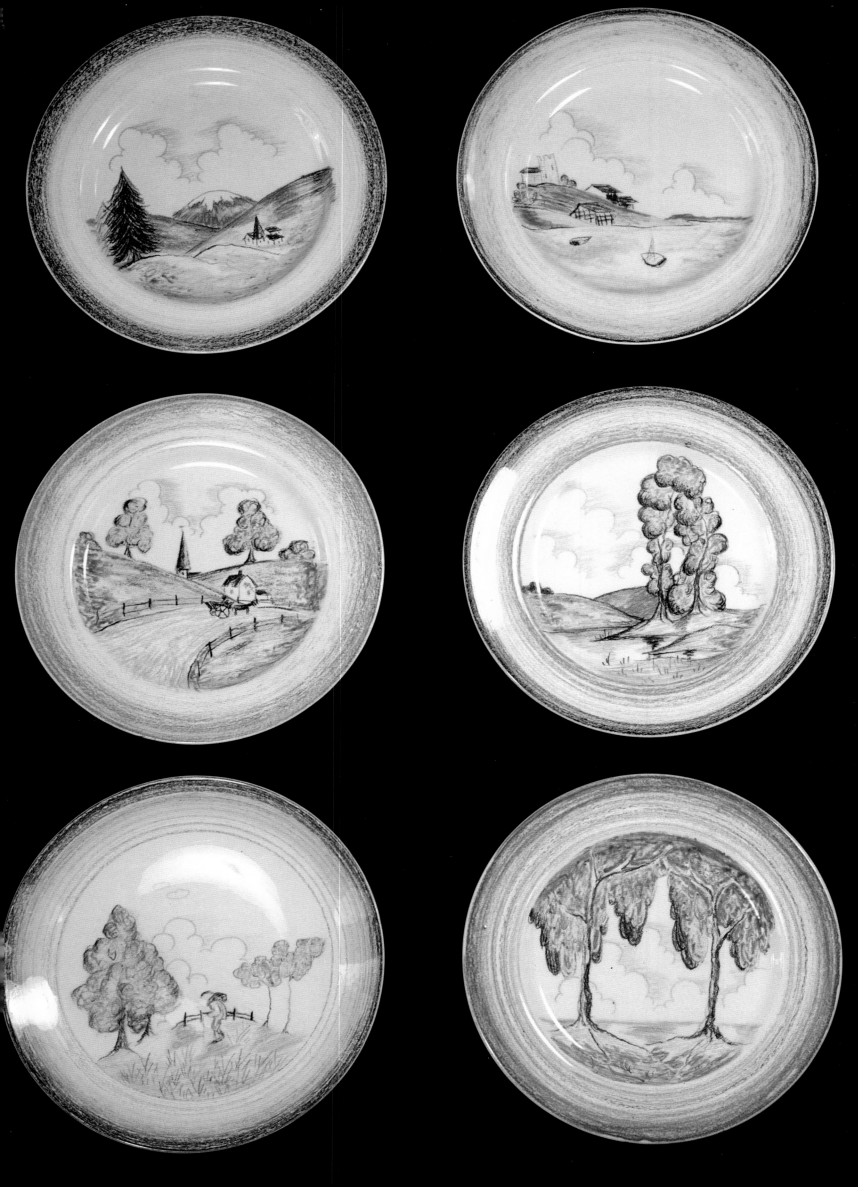

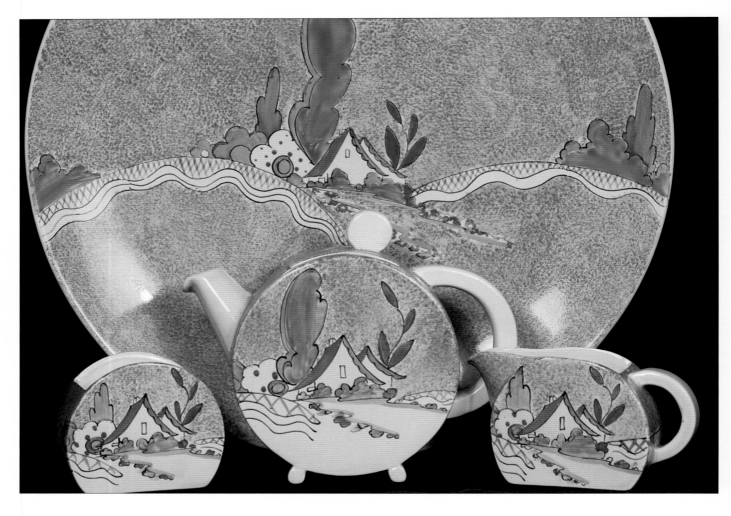

the shape appeared in August 1929, many stockists could only be supplied with old traditional teaware as late as December.

One consequence of so many *Early Morning sets*, in so many designs, selling in a short space of time was that, when unpacking them, sales staff at the stores sometimes mixed up the saucers or lids. Customers then unknowingly bought a set with some pieces that were not theirs. Often the first they knew of this was when they tried to sell these treasured pieces of Clarice Cliff forty or fifty years later. It seems from advertisements of the time that sets were also available made up from different designs.

Another stunning piece to appear in 1929 was made for Clarice by a technical apprentice Ron Birks. This obviously involved time in the *Bizarre* shop as apart from doing some stylised industrial designs on *Latona* glaze plates, he was allowed to model a large face mask. It was fifteen inches high, with features inspired by a mixture of Cubism and African tribal art. The result, suitably called *Grotesque*, was initially issued in *Inspiration* glazes. Despite a rather limited commercial appeal, its eye-catching shape at exhibitions meant it remained in production in various designs until at least 1937. Ron Birks signed the few plates he decorated on the front. The early masks have an impressed "RB" mark on the side but this is missing from later examples.

Before the end of September the *Fantasque* range was enlarged, new designs included *Fruit, Geometric Flowers, Sunrise* and *Umbrellas & Rain*. These nearly all featured Clarice's favourite bright orange and jade colours, and vivid banding. Teamed up with the mass of shapes she had made in her *Conical* series they attracted healthy sales.

At the same time as the *Fantasque* range was growing Clarice was adding to *Bizarre*. Startling new designs appeared between August and November 1929. These included *Sunray, Sliced Circle, Lightning, Diamonds, Mondrian, Football*, and surprisingly a landscape, *Luxor*. Seemingly simple designs such as *Football* are actually complex. The horizontal and vertical lines are in panels. Produced in strong orange, green, yellow and blue it is a classic Clarice Cliff abstract. *Sunray* has black skyscraper shapes, stunning purple and orange sun, and stars in a yellow sky. Some collectors still call it *Night & Day* even though the original name has been discovered.

Blue 'W' a new *Fantasque* design appeared shortly after this. It defies description; in a mass of overlapping shapes and colours, the part of the design from which the name was chosen is the only orthodox part.

All these designs were in the classic Art Deco style which has made them very collectable since, but they seem to have been in production for less than a year when issued.

Two of the most Cubist-inspired designs appeared at this time. Not knowing the original name, one has been named *Cubist* after the painting movement that inspired it, and another called *Orange/Blue Squares*. These designs share the same colours of orange, blue, green and yellow, delineated with a strong black outline. Whilst we find such pieces stunning today, they were clearly only made briefly, in small erratic batches for six months. Examples are found with both the early *Bizarre* and *Fantasque* backstamps, so even the factory did not know what range they were in.

The promotion of her new products became an all-consuming passion for Clarice. She devised a format for the demonstrations; adding visual impact by getting the factory woodworkers to build special display material for *Bizarre*, and arranged for the girls to wear artist's smocks and floppy bows as they decorated.

From the 27th of September Clarice and Colley staged a major promotion at the *China, Earthenware and Pottery Exhibition* at the First Avenue Hotel in London. It attracted a lot of press attention and the contrast between Clarice and Colley's comments shows their very different visions of the same project. Colley Shorter was quoted as saying,

"*England is today reaping the benefit of years of scientific and practical research, and the accumulated and inherited skill of generations of craftsmen and craftswomen.*"

Clarice's comments were more specific.

Top:
Chalet
Clarice Cliff
1936-1937
Colourful flower beds by a path leading to a chalet, against a green *Cafe-au-Lait* style sky.
★★★★£££

Bottom left:
Bowling
Bizarre
1929
Random horizontal banding with freehand bulls-eye motif.
★★★★£££

Bottom right:
Branch & Squares
Bizarre
1930
Outlined black, orange or blue leaves on a branch enclosed in irregular squares, painted in unclassifiable random colours.
★★★★£££
See also *Flower & Squares*.

"*Initially it was a difficult task in trying to persuade the buyers (from the stores) to take up this modern pottery. It was not until women buyers appeared that it was realised that women wanted bright and cheerful pottery in their homes, rather than the old-fashioned styles of circles of roses, and elaborate gold lines and decorations.*"

The last few months of 1929 also saw the launch of sophisticated designs for tableware and tea and coffee-ware. The *Moderne* range showed the French influence in more than its name; designs were just small square motifs set on the corner or edge of ware, with simple lining on part of the body. This was clearly influenced by what Clarice experienced in Paris. A *Conical* teaset in a *Moderne* design made a fashionable present. The shape of the ware and use of a cartouche to hold the design motif pre-dates the similarly styled *Vogue* and *Mode* Eric Slater issued for Shelley Potteries in 1930.

It is hard to believe that having achieved so much in under a year that Clarice did anything other than spend every day at work, however, we know from contemporary press coverage, that she attended numerous exhibitions, and looked after her Bizarre girls as they went on more successful demonstrations. Generally Clarice accompanied them, or at least saw them off from the railway station, and she ensured they had good accommodation. Clarice usually went down for the London trips, at one of these Mary Brown demonstrated banding and was pictured at the wheel in national newspapers. However, as the factory was so busy she had to demonstrate by herself. Clarice rewarded Mary by taking her out on an open-top bus to see the sights, followed by a meal.

Mary Brown and all the other girls had not realised when they joined that working as a hand-paintress for Clarice Cliff would mean paid trips all over Britain. The trips were regarded as a treat, few of them had ever travelled so far. The stories of their adventures would be told to the other girls as they gossiped merrily whilst painting - tales of visits to the British Museum, or the London Odeon, would only pause if Miss Cliff or Mr. Colley happened to walk through the Bizarre shop.

This page:
Cherry
Fantasque
1929
Blue coloured berries and purple leaves with orange detail, outlined in green, it was originally *Fantasque* 102.
★★★★£££

Opposite:
Cubist
Bizarre
1929-1930
An extremely strong abstract design of interlocking geometric shapes in orange, blue, green, black and yellow. Although it would have been a straight forward design to paint, very few examples appear to have been produced.
Contemporary to Carpet this design like Café, Mondrian and Orange/Blue Squares was copied from the work of the Dutch 'De Stijl' movement. Without doubt it is based on Theo van Doesburg's 1924 painting 'Counter Compostion V'.
★★★★££££

Top:

Car & Skyscraper
Bizarre
1933
Outlined design of exaggerated skyscrapers with a long sleek car in front. This design was a sample produced by one of Clarice's outliners Harold Walker, the drawing for it is in his Burslem School of Art design books.

Bottom and page 18:

Clouvre
Inspiration
1930-1931
An *Inspiration* ground with freehand on glaze hand-painted designs. Variations include *Water Lily*, *Butterfly* and *Tulip*.
★★★★★£££

Opposite:

Diamonds
Bizarre
1929-1930
A very bold abstract/geometric design consisting of two adjacent panels. One is a simple diamond shape, the other with square, curved and circular motifs. The colours used were black, blue, orange and yellow but a few examples are known with some of the elements painted green instead of blue. In early pieces the panels are divided by a single vertical line but later this became a double line with the space betwen them either coloured in or left clear.
This design may have been an attempt by Clarice Cliff to emulate the style of the Dutch 'De Stijl' movement whose work she admired.
★★★★£££££

As she got busier Clarice needed more help, she recruited a warehouse worker Hilda Lovatt, to be her assistant. They got on well and were friends throughout their lives. A duty Hilda particularly enjoyed was keeping a scrap-book of cuttings from newspapers and magazines about Clarice and *Bizarre*. She maintained this until the middle of the Fifties. Despite their closeness, Hilda always called Clarice, Miss Cliff, even 40 years later.

This page:
Circles & Squares
Fantasque
1929-1930
A band of overlapping circles and squares each with a vertical line passing through the centre called 'Allsorts' in Australia.
★★★★★£££

Opposite:
Double 'V'
Bizarre
1929
Black and yellow 'V's dividing panels of orange, blue and green abstract shapes. Various other colour combinations with slight variations in the detail of the design were also produced.
★★★★££££

CHAPTER 4

1930
A RUNAWAY SUCCESS

Clarice demonstrated her liberal approach to life when she moved out of the family home at Edward Street, Tunstall. She took a flat above a hairdressers at Snow Hill, Hanley. A single woman living alone was somewhat unorthodox. The girls were shocked by this and heard that it had resulted in a blazing row between Clarice and her sister Dolly. It was unlikely that she could maintain this flat on the wages she earned, this further fuelling speculation about her and Colley Shorter.

In the little time Clarice was away from the factory she gradually furnished and decorated the flat; the few colleagues who were invited around remember its colour. The bathroom walls and ceiling were covered in shiny yellow and black paper, it had a pink and blue bedroom, the chairs were all painted white.

In the first few months of the year Colley Shorter had put the entire work's staff at her disposal for the British Industries Fair in February. The works managers, painters and engineers all assisted in the design and manufacture of display stands. Everything was assembled at the factory by Bill Taylor and Sam Hilditch under Clarice's supervision, then transported by lorry to London. There, Clarice and Hilda Lovatt would spend several days arranging things, just before the opening Clarice would personally choose masses of fresh flowers to arrange in her vases.

Bizarre stands at the British Industries Fair, the Ideal Home Exhibition, and at gift and fancy goods fairs in Blackpool, Harrogate and Manchester, became annual

Bottom left:
Brunella
Fantasque
1929-1930
A freehand stylised floral motif in a rust and blue, similar to the Ravel design.
★★★★£

Bottom right:
Buttercup
Bizzare
1932
Cafe-au-Lait all over design in green, yellow and red combined. Teaware has orange handles. Known with purple body and blue handles.
★★★££

Opposite:
Etna
Appliqué
1931
A volcanic peak in the distance, in the foreground a blue sea, with black rocky cliffs covered with green trees.
★★★★★£££££

events. Colley Shorter was the force behind these events, he realised that *Bizarre* was the most saleable product he had ever had. Consequently he ensured the stands stimulated a lot of newspaper and magazine coverage.

The largest pieces made as a standard part of the *Bizarre* range were chargers and umbrella stands. Chargers were initially eighteen inches in diameter, and cast as it was not possible to press such a large shape from solid clay. They were ribbed to give them strength and although all have holes drilled in a foot rim, were designed to be used both on a wall and as a table centrepiece. This is why some designs were produced radially. The factory also made large vases and umbrella stands. These cost between twenty two shillings in a *Bizarre* design and forty four shillings in an *Inspiration* one. At this time the *Bizarre* girls weekly wage was around seven shillings and eight pence.

The range of colours used on Clarice's ware was to increase dramatically during 1930. There was a considerable difference in cost between some colours, which is why ranges such as *Latona* and *Appliqué* were more expensive. The two main suppliers of the powder colour were Harrison's and Blythe's. The early pieces had been limited to a narrow palette, dominated by the rusty red called Harrison's Red so common on original *Bizarre*. This was used extensively in the early years as it was inexpensive and easy to apply. To improve the look of the ware, however, Clarice almost completely dropped it during early 1930 in favour of a brighter colour called Coral Red. This had a dramatic effect on the impact of her designs, but Jim Hall remembers that it cost four times as much as Harrison's Red. The result was that many designs which started out using lots of Coral Red soon had it replaced with Clarice's favourite shiny orange. The orange colour was more durable and easier for the paintresses to apply, and this is why it is found on so many designs. The Coral Red was then used sparingly for just detail on a design or occasionally on sample pieces for trade shows. Various makes of blue enamel were tried as this colour was difficult to fire. The shiny perfect blue that was used on a few *Appliqué* designs early in 1930 was too expensive for general use, and the factory persisted in using No. 5 blue which caused problems.

This page:
Clovelly
Clarice Cliff
1937
Red-roofed houses leading to the sea, with a small island in the distance. Produced with pen outline, also pattern number 6932.
★★★★££

Opposite:
Inspiration Caprice
1929-1931
A landscape with fir trees and a bridge with decorative pillars either end.
★★★£££££
See also hand-painted *Caprice*.

Opposite:
Inspiration Rose
1930
A large pink rose, with yellow outlining and blue and lilac leaves.
★★★★££££

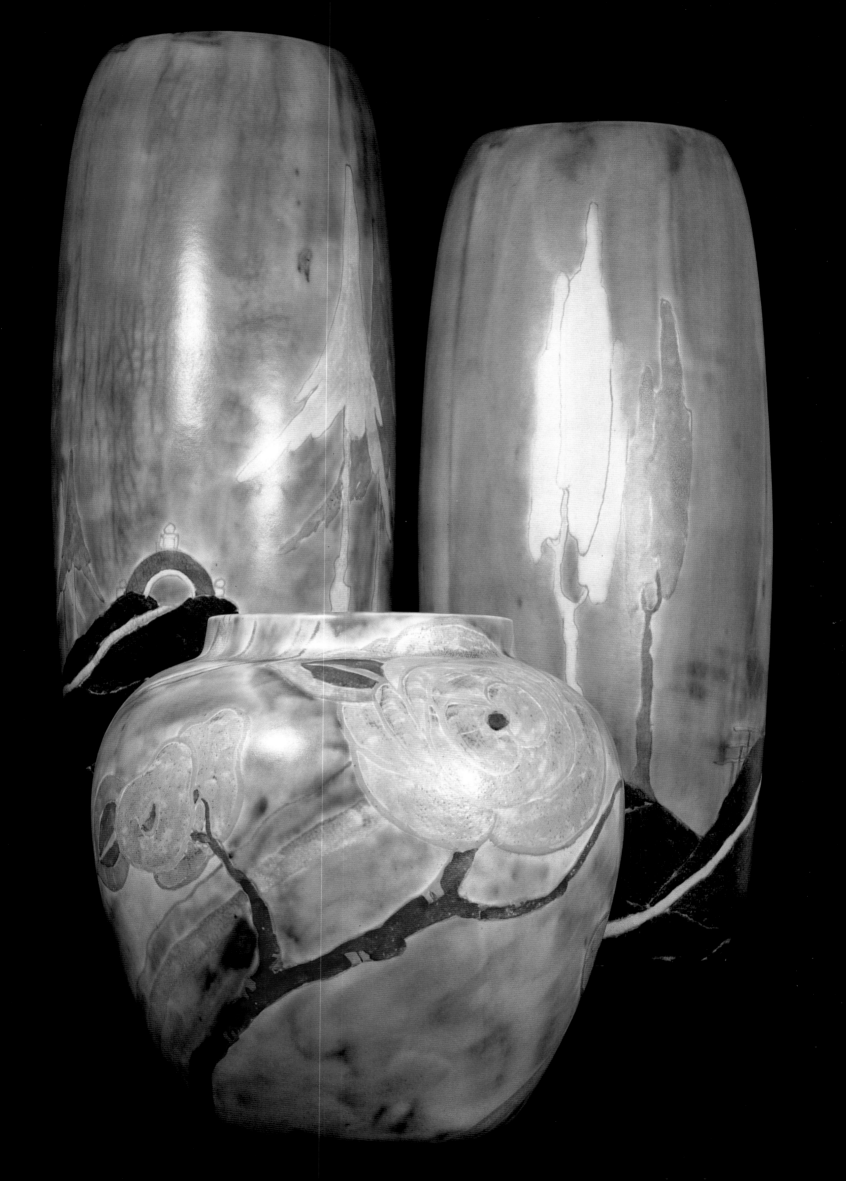

Bottom left:
Cabbage Flower
Bizarre
1934
Green and grey flowers, red and grey leaves growing from brown earth against a woven yellow sky.
★★★£

Bottom right:
Cherry Blossom
Clarice Cliff
1935-1936
Red and green *Delecia* style runnings with a delicate tree painted over them, with small white blossoms, produced by rubbing the wet paint with a fingertip.
★★★££

Top:
Crepe de Chine
Bizarre
1933
An all over floral design, with printed outline in black, hand enamelled in green yellow and blue.
★★★★££

Opposite:
Farmhouse
Fantasque
1931-1932 (matchings to 1935)
A cottage with a ground to roof level chimney, amidst trees and bushes, in brown, orange and green.
Also known on an Inspiration glaze.
★★★★££££

All the new paintresses had to spend time learning how to mix the powdered colour with fat-oil and turps. They did this for their own use and for the more experienced paintresses. The Coral Red went on very thickly, whereas the purple was a difficult colour to apply evenly and *Bizarre* girl Cissy Rhodes recalled, "Miss Cliff said I was always to do the purple". Lessons learnt about using the colours in the early days meant that by 1930 the technical quality of the on-glaze colours was considerably better than when original *Bizarre* started.

Key new designs appeared at this time that were to prove successful for several years, and we now look back at them as being quintessential Clarice Cliff. *Melon* and *Trees & House* were added to the *Fantasque* range, and colourways and variations of existing designs appeared. *Sunburst* was a more sophisticated version of the early *Bizarre* with triangles forming a star shape in Coral Red, orange, yellow and brown.

Trees & House was Clarice's first successful landscape, being more formalised than the earlier *Caprice* and *Luxor* designs. The source of it seems to be an ink sketch (sample 524) in the Newport Pottery samples book dated the 31st May 1929, so the design developed in 1929. However, the sketch was much simpler than the production pattern, so there was probably an intermediate stage, this could have been the *Pastel Trees & House* colourway. It is likely that the design was only put into regular production in early 1930.

Trees & House was decorated in Coral Red in early 1930, but then was mainly done with orange, which complemented the jade and black. The design was adaptable as the elements could easily be shortened or lengthened to fit various shapes. The *Pastel Trees & House* with seven colours, was also issued briefly, most examples seem to have been exported to the Commonwealth countries; its consequent rarity has made it very collectable. The orange colourway then continued in production right through until 1933.

Melon was a more significant design. Influenced by a Cubist Picasso painting, Clarice added her favourite orange and jade to a palette of rust, yellow and blue to produce

Bottom left:
Christine
Tableware
1934
A central printed floral motif, with hand-painted hatching around edge. Colourways blue, yellow and brown.
★★★£

Bottom right:
Coastal Oak
Bizarre
1934
A thinly drawn freehand coastal landscape with a stylised tree with a few very large red and brown oak leaves.
★★★★★££

Opposite:
Gayday
Bizarre
1930-1934
Orange, rust red, and purple asters, amidst green leaves, all painted freehand, between brown, green and yellow bands.
★££
See also *Sungay*.

Opposite:
Sungay
Bizarre
1932-1933
Asters in yellow, blue and green. This was loosely based on *Gayday*, hence its name.
★★★£££
See also *Gayday*.

Top:
Crest
Bizarre
1933
A black and red crest motif, against a
ground of overlapping crescent shapes in
blue and green.
★★★★★£££

Crocus
1928 -1963
Freehand *Crocus* flowers with thin green
leaves produced in a number of variations.
*All examples can be partly dated by the
backstamp, just a Clarice Cliff mark is post
1936, with "Royal Staffordshire Ceramics"
post 1952.*

Opposite:
Autumn Crocus
Bizarre
1928-1963
Flowers in orange, blue and purple.
★££

Bottom:
Sungleam Crocus
Bizarre
1931-1934
Orange and yellow flowers.
★★★£££

a design that was unique. The contour line effect between the stylised fruit also gave a cohesive element to it. It remained in production for three years, several colourways were produced during that time, the rarest of which is *Melon Red*.

One misunderstanding that has built up over the years is that Clarice Cliff ware was sold at Woolworth's. We know from managers at Newport Pottery that the cost of hand-painted ware was far too expensive. The reality was that by 1930 Clarice Cliff was selling to Harrods and also producing a design unique to them. Incorporated into the backstamp on the ware was *Exclusive to Harrods Knightsbridge London SW1*, and underneath this, *Doré by Clarice Cliff*.

Early in 1930 yet another new decoration was added to the *Bizarre* range. Clarice reverted to a style that had been present in the Staffordshire Potteries for over a hundred years. Powder colour mixed thinly with turps was run over the ware, by using complementary colours this produced pleasing results. With her characteristic flair for creating names for her ware, Clarice chose *Delecia*.

After a few experiments Clarice realised that her paintresses could achieve reasonably consistent results. Clarice chose Elsie Nixon and Winnie Davis to do this decoration. As the process was a messy one, they were given a separate shop where the ware was produced. The decoration involved painting the watery colours around the shape, allowing them to run over each other, then fanning them with a piece of card to dry before the effect was overdone. This meant that Elsie often ended-up covered in colour, she remembers Clarice saying with a smile, "You're a dirty worker Elsie, but you get the results!"

As well as doing *Delecia*, Elsie was trained by Clarice to assist in her photographic studio and darkroom. Clarice and Hilda Lovatt arranged the ware on display stands and took the pictures under two strong lights, which created quite fierce shadows giving some of her pictures a cinema-noir quality. Using shiny surfaces to stand the ware on gave the photography an Art Deco feel. Elsie was taught how to develop and print the black and white films, and remembers that on winter days the room was so

Bottom left:
Blue Crocus
Bizarre
1935
All the flowers in shades of blue.
★★★£££

Opposite:
Forest Glen
Bizarre and Clarice Cliff
1935-1937
A green etched hill side with a pen outline cottage in the middle distance under a deep red and grey sky produced in *Delecia* runnings. Was also known as pattern number 6614.
★★★£££
See also *Newlyn*.

Opposite:
Newlyn
Bizarre and Clarice Cliff
1935-1937
A green etched hill side with a pen outline cottage in the middle distance under a grey and blue sky produced in *Delecia* runnings.
★★★£££
See also *Forest Glen*.

Bottom right:
Purple Crocus
Bizarre
1935
All the flowers in shades of purple.
★★★★★££££

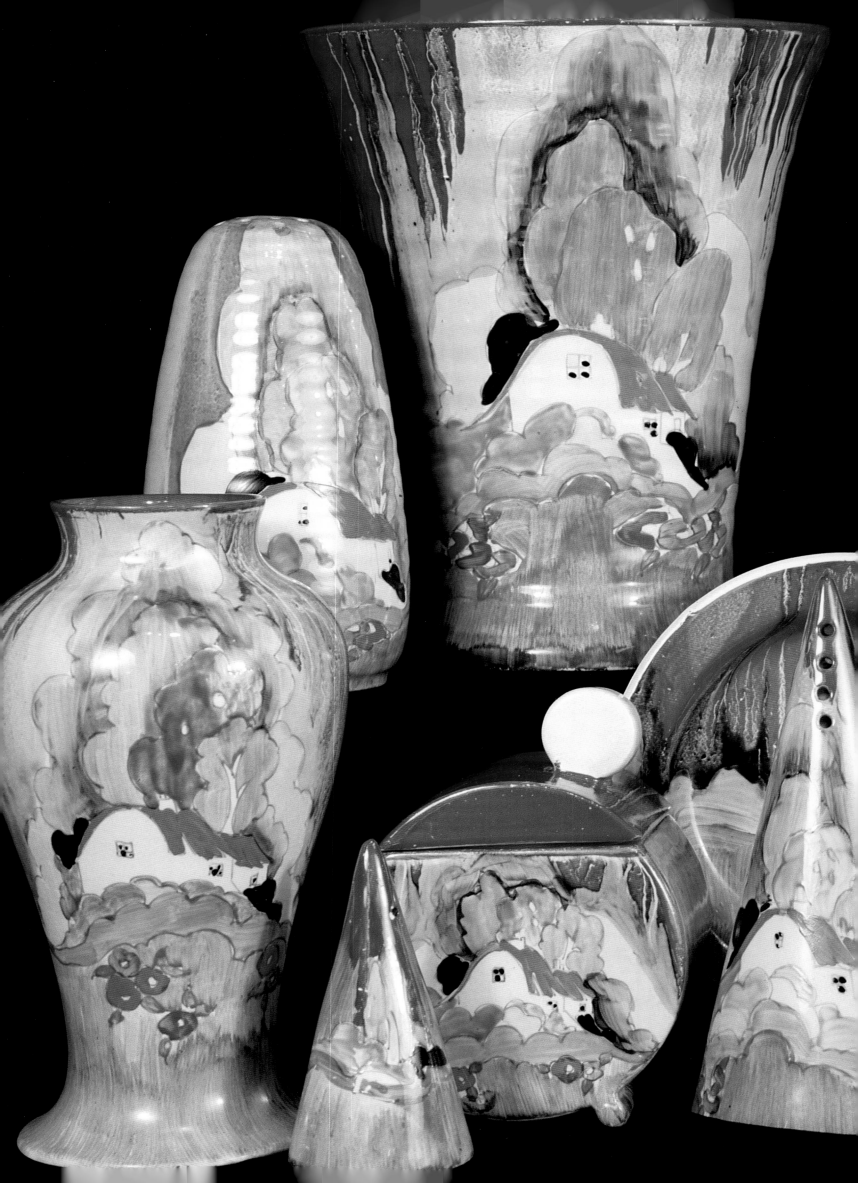

cold that some of the liquids used had frozen in the[ir] containers!

The *Delecia* range was executed on some of Clarice['s] new *Conical* shapes, but also on traditionally shaped ware, including some of the re[m]aining stock of *Archaic* shapes. The ware sold reasonably, but for some reason its [p]roduction seems to have been discontinued. Perhaps the factory had such a varie[ty] of shapes and designs by this time that it was finding it difficult to administrate t[he]m? However, the *Delecia* name was later to be revived. Immediately after *Delecia* C[la]rice did the trial pieces of what has since become one of her most significant range[s]. Again showing her preference for French names, the range was called *Appliqué*.

This was not simply a series of designs, but the name of a new technique for producing them. The outline was done in Indian ink [in] the usual way. When the pieces were fired, the ink [b]urnt away leaving the colours against each other. The other characteristic of *App[liq]ué* was that Clarice used more colours on it than *Bizarre* or *Fantasque*, some of the[se] were exclusive to the range. The extra time needed to decorate the ware and [the] more expensive colours, made *Appliqué* a more prestigious series. All *Appliqué* desig[n]s were distinguished by having strong banding of black, Coral Red, black, and in s[o]me cases a central yellow band. This gave the ware even more impact.

Clarice seems to have initially intended *Appliqué* [t]o be a landscape series using continental names as the inspiration for scenes. It w[a]s launched with two scenes in March 1930: *Lucerne* featured a castle in a mo[un]tainous landscape; *Lugano*, a waterwheel on a hillside. Both featured all-over co[lo]ur with deep blue skies. They had a lot more impact than the simpler *Bizarre* desig[ns] they were contemporary with. However, sales do not appear to have gone well, [wi]thin two months Clarice had adapted them so the sky was orange and the desig[ns] started to appear on all her shapes.

Further *Appliqué* designs in the middle of 1930 inclu[d]ed *Avignon*, a blue bridge in an ornamental garden with a lily pond; *Windmill*, whic[h] featured the building in deep

This page:
Damask Rose
Bizarre
1931-1932
A body produced by mixing slip with a pink colourant. Once cast and fired the biscuit ware pieces were then given a clear glaze. To allow the effect to show through it was decorated just with unclassified small fruit or floral motifs painted freehand.
★★★££

Opposite:
Fragrance
Bizarre
1935
Tall delphiniums and a large tree in a country garden with small blue and pink flowers in the foreground all painted freehand.
★★★£££
See also *Sandon*.

Opposite:
Sandon
Bizarre
1935
A country garden with tall delphiniums, and a large tree, with flowers in the foreground in yellow and orange; named after a village near Stoke-on-Trent.
★★★££
See also *Fragrance*.

Opposite:
Trallee
See page 86.

This page:
Delecia Citrus
Bizarre
1932-34
Oranges and lemons above green and grey
runnings, with blue and green leaves.
A rare version has gold and silver fruit.
★★★£££

Opposite:
Garden
Appliqué
1931
A tree with light and dark blue foliage,
over a garden of orange, yellow and brown
flowers.
*A single example of an alternate colourway
has a brown and orange tree.*
★★★★★£££££

Page 85:
Trallee
Clarice Cliff
1935-1936
An etched thatched-roofed cottage with
window shutters, in a country garden, with
a *Cafe-au-Lait* blue smoke coming out of its
chimney.
★★★£££
See also *Sandon.*

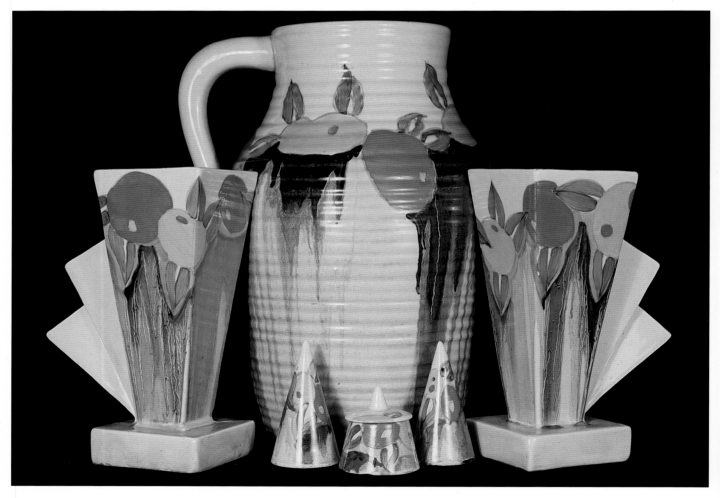

blue against an orange sky with red clouds. One of the rarest of the *Appliqué* designs issued at this time is *Garden*. This was unknown until 1988, but further examples have appeared which show it was produced with both a blue tree, and a brown and orange one. Of the three known examples of *Appliqué Garden* two came from Scotland implying that it was perhaps a sample design that never went into full production.

As the in-store demonstrations continued some of the girls also got paid to go away. Sadie Maskrey, Annie Beresford, Gladys Scarlett and Ellen Browne went to Lawley's in Regent Street, London from the 2nd to the 7th of June.

This visit to London was one of the first times Clarice was quoted in the national press. The journalist noted, "Chatting with Miss Cliff about her achievements is in itself a delightful experience. She is so modest about it all, claiming no special personal merit for the happy revelation she has brought about." Clarice's actual words give us an insight into how she perceived her work and her inspirations.

"*Very tentatively at first I set to work, moulding new patterns, developing new and daring decorations. Ideas borrowed from meadow flowers, from gems, from bits of bright enamel as were produced by old Italian craftsmen... Everything with a touch of orange in it, I had noticed seemed to take people's fancy, while jade green was another 'winning' colour. At first I had about a dozen boys and girls carrying out my designs. Now over 200 are employed just on the decorating alone and with the steady increase in popularity in bright modern pottery for table use, more and more work is being found for both beginners and more experienced workers.*"

Although Clarice exaggerated the number of *Bizarre* decorators which was normally about sixty at this time, Marjory Higginson recalled that one day in the early Thirties, intrigued to know how many staff were decorating for Clarice, she counted all the paintresses and the four boy outliners. She visited the various shops on the Newport site, and counted eighty. This included decorators temporarily moved across from Wilkinson's when Newport staff could not keep up with demand. Taking into account

Bottom left:
Devon
Bizarre
1933
A pendulous red tree, with garden of stylised flowers underneath, in orange green and blue.
★★★★££££
See also *Moonlight*.

Bottom right:
Dore
Bizarre
1930
Printed outline of an oblong with an abstract design, and a floral motif over one side. Produced exclusively for Harrods.
★★★★££

Opposite:
Gardenia
Fantasque
1931-1932
A large central orange or coral red flower with smaller blue and purple ones amidst green and black leaves.
Colourways:
Orange ★★★£££
Red ★★★££££

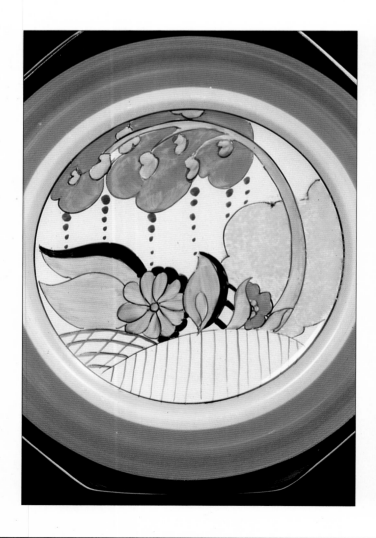

aerographers, and lithographers at Wilkinson's perhaps Clarice quoted the staff in all the decorating processes on both sites?

Clarice's reply when the journalist asked her if she had been influenced by foreign examples is interesting.

"Not to any larger extent I have only really visited one foreign country - France - and that for the briefest of holidays. I admire the work of foreign potters but as far as my designs are concerned I can claim that they are English right through."

Clarice's last claim was only partly true, as we know that she hoarded a mass of books in her studio at Newport and she was certainly aware of the designs of Edouard Benedictus. She had a prodigious thirst for knowledge about design and a lot of the girls remember her forever studying her books looking for inspiration. The foreign potters Clarice said she admired clearly included Lallemant, but some shapes she issued in 1931 demonstrated that she also knew of the work of others.

New floral designs were introduced continually. *Gayday* had large colourful aster flowers in the same palette as *Melon*, and these were mainly painted by Winnie Pound and Ivy Stringer. *Crocus* continued to sell extremely well, as demand grew it was necessary to set up a *Crocus* shop on the floor beneath the *Bizarre* shop. Five or six teams sat at benches painting nothing else, week after week. To relieve the tedium they sang or chatted, but Clarice thought they worked harder when they were quiet, so an early warning system was devised to announce her imminent arrival. As her routine was to go from her studio, into the *Bizarre* shop, then to the *Crocus* shop, Marjory Higginson upstairs would drop a stilt through a gap in the floorboards which would fall noisily into a saucer placed strategically on a bench below. This clatter instantly subdued the *Crocus* girls who Clarice was always pleased to find were hard at work. However, several early paintresses recalled that the repetitive nature of doing only *Crocus*, eventually led them to leave to work elsewhere.

To cope with increased demand, the *Bizarre* shop was extended into the area near Clarice's studio, making it 'L' shaped, now held up to sixty decorators. There was a team spirit present in the shops, they were becoming aware that being a Clarice Cliff girl meant something in the Potteries.

The routine in the *Bizarre* shop was well established by this time, and May Keeling recounted how the day began.

"We arrived at 8.00 and went to our benches and got our colours ready. You would have your work there from the previous day. Lily Slater would tell you what to do. A little later Colley Shorter would walk through with the mail under his arm, and Clarice would follow. We could not help but notice that Mr. Colley beamed at her and she could do no wrong."

May was one of the paintresses who left in 1932 after being on *Crocus* for a year. However, enameller Sadie Maskrey who had moved to the *Bizarre* shop in 1929 from Wilkinson's, enjoyed her work enamelling samples.

"When I did samples I still worked in the Bizarre shop. Ellen Browne traced, I coloured them in doing all the colours. I would copy from a drawing. John Shaw and Harold Walker did the outlining on some pieces I decorated, they did larger pieces. Samples took more time and had more careful brushstrokes. Clarice had the samples when they came out of the kiln and passed them on to the travellers. We put our initial on the back, mine was an 'S' mark."

Clarice Cliff's *Age of Jazz* figures first "danced" into view in the summer of 1930. The idea of producing sleek cut-out figures of dancing couples and musicians, playing and dancing to a Jazz Age tune is a world away from the solid clay figures Clarice had made six years previously. The influences she had absorbed in the intervening years gave her a whole new perspective on design, but with these pieces she excelled herself. Some of the girls have suggested that Clarice may have been inspired to produce these because her sister Dolly, a keen dancer, gave demonstrations of dancing in Stoke and appeared in shows at the Hippodrome.

The concept of a shape made as a silhouette and supported in a base was taken from

Opposite:
Football
Bizarre
1929-1930
An abstract wrap round design of four adjacent panels, each repeating the design in a higher or lower position. The black outline which is either horizontal or vertical varies in thickness and the colours are usually orange, purple, yellow and green with a net motif in blue cross hatching. A few colour variations are known but it is unlikely that they are intentional alternate colourways.
★★★★££££

Top:
Delecia
Delecia
1930-1931
The original *Delecia* effect was produced with raw colour mixed with turpentine which was allowed to run all over the ware leaving a pattern of randomly coloured drips.
★★£££££

Bottom:
Delecia Daisy
Bizarre
1932
Blue and pink flowers, with purple etching.
★★£££

Bottom:
Delecia Pansies
Bizarre
1932-1934
This has the same flowers as the *Nasturtium* design, but in pastel shades with *Delecia* runnings under the flowers.
★★★£££

Bottom:
Delecia Poppy
Bizarre
1932-1933
Large flowers in red, yellow and purple.
★★★£££

Opposite:
Gibraltar
See page 95.

some trees produced in this style by Robert Lallemant, that Clarice found in *Mobilier et Décoration*. However, apart from this the figures were original and certainly a more imaginative use of the idea than Lallemant's. Again Bill Lunt's department found itself stretched to produce the shape as she originally designed it. Some of the original dancers snapped easily as the waist was too slim. They were given a thicker middle, and Clarice added a spray of flowers down the dress to distract from the more ample figure.

The set of five pieces consisted of three dancing couple figurines, one of which had two couples, a fourth had a drummer and saxophonist, the final piece was a guitarist and piano player. They were all in bow-ties and evening gowns. The outlining on the figures was a print rather than hand-painted, so both sides corresponded at the edge. There seems to be no standard colouring as on the double figure the dresses are known in orange and green, red and yellow, green and yellow, and one lady even has green hair! They were sold individually boxed and one of Clarice's atmospheric photographs of them casting long shadows was included inside the lid. Clarice said that the *Age of Jazz* figures were, "To be used as table centre-pieces for dinner parties whilst listening to the radio."

The *Age of Jazz* figures proved attention getting and Clarice was pictured in the press decorating them at the First Avenue Hotel in London. It was unimportant that sales were not good, as their primary function was to attract publicity. The lack of sales then is contrasted by an amazing interest in them now, and this coupled with their rarity has made them consistently expensive.

At the same time as the *Age of Jazz* figures were produced, Clarice's *Stamford* teapot appeared. In contrast it sold extremely well. It was issued to complement the *Conical* shape teaware. The teapot's flat sides caused problems in the modelling stage, and Clarice liaised with Joe Woolliscroft, the head modeller, until they got it right. Joe was remembered by other staff as a genial gentlemen, who was excellent in his highly skilled job of making the blocks and cases for the moulds. They recall that he had to put up with Clarice's demands, but maintained his integrity. Away from work he relaxed by playing bassoon in the North Staffordshire Symphony Orchestra.

Unlike the *Conical* teapot Clarice did copy the *Stamford* shape. The original had been made in 1925 by Tétard Frères, well-known French silversmiths. Basing ceramic designs on silver or metalware was a tradition in the Potteries, so Clarice would have had no qualms about copying this shape. In this case we know that Tétard Frères did object to the copy, but in 1932 some of the brothers from the company visited Newport Pottery and after heated negotiations supplied further shapes to Clarice for which they were paid.

In an interview in 1930, Clarice clearly had a focused idea of her market.

"*Women today want continual change... they will have colour and plenty of it... colour seems to radiate happiness and the spirit of modern life and movement, and I cannot put too much of it into my designs to please women.*"

However, aware of Colley Shorter's thriftiness she attempted to reduce the cost of putting colour in her designs at this time. Clarice experimented to see if it was possible to capture the style of *Bizarre* by replacing the hand-painted outlining process with a print of the design which was then enamelled and banded as normal. Designs produced by this method included *Solomon's Seal*, *Nemesia*, and *Flora*. Response from retailers and customers was not favourable, *Bizarre* designs thankfully remained hand-painted.

The ever increasing demand for *Bizarre* meant that Clarice took on yet more new paintresses, including her own sister Ethel, who was a bander and liner and also worked in the warehouse. Factories in Stoke-on-Trent often employed people from the same family. Ethel Barrow's sister Lily joined the *Crocus* shop, as did Fred Ridgway's daughters Beryl and Audrey, as well as Marjory Higginson's sister Dorothy. Other new girls at this time were Jessie MacKenzie, Gladys Birkin, Nora Dabbs, and Alice Andrews who was eventually to work quite closely with Clarice Cliff. Alice recalls:

Bottom left:
Dryday
Clarice Cliff
1937
A thinly drawn brown freehand tree with green leaves. White egg shaped flowers below.
★★£

Bottom right:
Eating Apples
Clarice Cliff
1937
Yellow and red apples with green and grey pears overlapping with leaf shapes, outlined in a fine black line.
★★★★★££

Top:
Eden
Appliqué
1931
A brown flower surrounded by black flowers, green leaves with black veins, with a glimpse of an orange sky, with a blue and green landscape in the background.
★★★★★££££

Page 93:
Gibraltar
Fantasque
1931-1932
White-sailed yachts on a blue sea before the Rock of Gibraltar in pink, lilac and green.
The yacht motif was also used on tableware in the mid-thirties in a silver outline with no colour.
★★★£££££

"*My earliest memory is of Clarice wandering around with a white overall on that she never fastened! She was quite friendly but if she found a decorator had painted a piece badly she was quite critical.*"

The factory was so successful by the end of 1930 that it was necessary to organise and rationalise various parts of the production. The glost and biscuit warehouses had to store all the new shapes Clarice had produced. Additionally many old shapes were being revised, as covered in *Bizarre* and *Fantasque* designs they proved saleable to customers who liked a traditional shape in a modern design. The older shapes, with numbers 100 to 300, were reduced drastically, to the ones more suited to take *Bizarre* patterns. At the same time some old Wilkinson's and Newport Pottery shapes, some of which had been Clarice's work anyway, were re-numbered. This meant that whereas shapes 432 to 436 were the contemporary *Age of Jazz* figures, the 431 was the *Girl candlestick* dating from 1925. Old modelled figures of a *Dutch man* and *woman*, an *Orange seller* and *Match seller* dating from the mid-Twenties were also revived and confusingly added to the shape sheets with new numbers.

This may have enabled the staff to organise their sales more efficiently in 1930, but it causes a great deal of confusion for collectors who are tempted to assume that the number sequence is chronological - it is not.

It is hard to believe that so much was happening at Newport Pottery at the same time, but we know that Clarice often worked late two or three nights a week, paying one of her girls to keep her company. She clearly threw herself into her work even when she had achieved success. The fact that Colley Shorter had made her Art Director of Newport by this time explains how she was able to have so many people working under her.

As well as issuing new shapes and designs Clarice was able to adapt and develop existing lines; for instance the *Conical* teapot was made in four and six cup sizes. She also issued a new tea and coffee shape based on a tubular body with a square lid;

This page:
Elizabethan Cottage
Clarice Cliff
1937
An outlined and etched design with red roofed cottage with leaded windows half hidden by a thick green, blue and yellow wood.
★★★★££

Opposite:
Green Firs
Bizarre
1934
Green and yellow fir trees in a blue and yellow landscape, the rarest colourway of *Blue* and *Coral Firs*.
★★★★★£££££
See also *Blue Firs* and *Coral Firs*.

Bottom:
Erin
Bizarre
1933-1934
Cloud shaped bushes with egg-shaped devices floating in the sky above.
Colourways:
Orange ★★★£££
Green ★★★★£££

Top:
Floreat
Bizarre
1929-1930
Orange flowers with green and clear leaves, with black details.
Referred to as Wild Rose in the archives.
★★★£££

Opposite:
Green House
Fantasque
1930
A green house with an orange roof, over which is bent a coral red, green and yellow tree.
★★★★★£££££
See also *Orange House.*

inspired by the academic mortar board. She fittingly called this *Eton*. However, the milk and sugar used were the ones from the *Conical* set and although produced until at least 1935, the shape appears to have been overlooked in favour of others. Consequently *Eton* is now quite rare and very collectable.

Further glaze experiments were undertaken, the *Gloria* range appeared and disappeared almost as quickly. This featured designs painted in water-colour on biscuit ware, which were then covered with the glaze, in the technique used by Poole Potteries in Dorset. *Inspiration* ware continued to be made and more sophisticated floral designs were issued, but the sheer cost of producing this ware led to its demise by 1932.

Existing ranges such as *Latona* and *Appliqué* had new designs added to them. New *Appliqué* designs issued late in 1930 included *Palermo*, based on the bay in Southern Italy, with yachts on the sea, and a colourful climbing plant in the foreground. *Appliqué Red Tree* had a surrealistic landscape that covered the ware in all-over colour. Before the end of the year *Bird of Paradise* was also issued but the one extant example implies this never got beyond the sample stage. *Caravan* is one of the few designs we actually have Clarice's comments on, from a contemporary newspaper article, when she was asked whether she found it difficult finding new ideas:

"*Some weeks are better than others. I got out twelve new designs last week, one of which is just coming out of the kiln. It introduces a Caravan under orange trees glowing with fruit, against a decorative background.*"

Apart from *Lucerne* and *Lugano*, the *Appliqué* designs all sold poorly when issued. This was perhaps a reflection of the fact that they were much more expensive, and that her customers preference at breakfast time was for the more homely *Gayday* or *Ravel*.

Other entirely new designs appeared in the second half of 1930. *Berries* was a well-balanced pattern with vivid red and orange berries, with yellow and green leaves. One of Clarice's most eye-catching landscapes appeared - *Green House* and *Orange House* were the colourways of the design that featured a tree tortuously blowing over the

This page:
Flower Music
Bizarre
1933
A simple design of sheet music with small petals as the notes.
★★★★★£

Opposite and page 1:
Honolulu
Bizarre
1933-1935
Stylised trees, with green and black mottled variegated trunks with pendulous red, orange and yellow foliage, and distinctive green banding with overlaid black lining.
★★★£££££
See also *Rudyard*.

roof of a strangely shaped house. It used the same stylised plant forms as *Trees & House* from which it was perhaps developed, but sold poorly.

A major new abstract appeared based on a design for a carpet by Ivan Da Silva Bruhns. The curved lines and dots of the picture Clarice saw in *Mobilier et Décoration* were purely in black and white. Clarice created her own colour scheme of red, black and grey, which was soon adapted to orange, black and grey. The original name was lost so in acknowledging its source it is called *Carpet*.

Inevitably, Clarice produced designs that were potentially good sellers, but for various reasons were overlooked. Her output at this time was prolific, and some rarer designs were probably only made in one trial batch. An example of this is one we have called *Sunspots*. It is a stunning mix of geometric shapes and dots in red, green, yellow and black. Stylistically we can relate this to *Carpet*, but today its value would be far greater because of its rarity.

It is worth remembering that all the work Clarice did during 1930 was done not just for artistic reasons, but to fight against the very serious effects of the depression. Her success provided secure full-time employment for her workers. One only needs to remember a story from *Bizarre* Girl Elsie Nixon to realise that life in the Potteries in 1930 was hard.

“*I was always late for work, but living at Ricardo Street next to Newport Pottery meant I could always run to work. I remember going past groups of barefoot young children. They hung around the factory gates in the hope of getting food. They shouted, 'We want cake missus, not bread', as I ran past them to try to get to work on time.*”

Opposite:
House & Bridge (Front cover)
Fantasque
1931-1933 (matchings until 1935)
A red-roofed cottage nestling at the bottom of a winding road, by a brown bridge, in the foreground is a tree with black trunk and pendulous orange, red and brown foliage.
★★★★££££

Bottom left:
'Bizarre Girls' Ellen Browne (left) and Sadie Maskrey were both outliners, and are here seen enjoying a chalet holiday together.

Bottom right:
Colley Shorter and Clarice never missed an opportunity to promote *Bizarre*. Here an entertainer endorses a *Bonjour* tea set.

CHAPTER 5

1931
THE PACE CONTINUES

Clarice Cliff, Colley Shorter and Newport Pottery steamed into 1931 with full order books, and were the most active potbank in Stoke-on-Trent, an area suffering twenty per cent unemployment at the time. The only hiccup was a brief strike over the tally system, for counting ware, but Mr. Colley had no intention of slowing down production so this was soon settled.

The *Fantasque* range grew dramatically throughout the year, and early in 1931 Clarice issued two new landscapes that became good sellers when issued and are now highly prized by collectors.

Autumn was another cottage in a landscape, but was distinguished by some stylish sinuous trees with bulbous foliage. Outlined in brown, the early samples seem to have continued the *Trees & House* tradition, being decorated in red, green and black. This was soon replaced with the most popular colourway, the foliage in dominant blue, with green and yellow and the bushes in purple. The production of this was initially standardised with chic banding of red, yellow and green, but as the design remained in regular production for three years, banding was subsequently issued in numerous colours. *Autumn* was so popular that a large number of colourways were produced in the following years, matchings were still being ordered as late as 1939.

Summerhouse was the other major design. Again outlined in brown it featured a tree with a green trunk, bright yellow foliage in a fantastic landscape dominated by a Coral Red summerhouse. The banding on this was more uniform, generally either

This page:
Flower Wave
Bizarre
1934
Yellow, blue and green flowers, with angled black stems, against a background of freehand blue wavy lines.
★★★★★£££

Opposite:
Idyll (Crinoline Lady)
Appliqué and Fantasque
1931-1936
A crinoline lady in a formal garden beneath a tree. Issued originally as an *Appliqué* design with black, red, black banding. Then with pastel banding and a more detailed dress it became a *Fantasque* design.
★★★£££

Clarice Cliff

Bottom left:
Ferndale
Clarice Cliff
1937
A tree with black trunk, yellow and brown etched foliage, and a red and yellow cottage and bushes in background.
★★★★£££

Bottom right:
Flora
Bizarre
1930
A print outline of buds, hand-painted in blue and orange.
Flora was also the name of a wallmask of a female head surrounded by flowers.
★★££

Top:
Flower & Squares
Bizarre
1930
The cubist flower from 'Picasso Flower' surrounded by overlapping squares painted in yellow, green, and purple.
★★★★★£££
See also *Branch & Squares.*

Opposite:
Limberlost
Bizarre
1932
A tree with a brown trunk and tan foliage, with large white flowers in the foreground, and green and brown bushes in the background.
★★★★£££

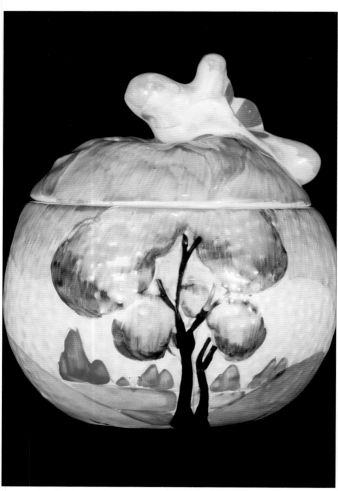

red or orange, and no other colourways were produced. It sold well, but in smaller quantities than *Autumn*, production was mainly limited to 1931 and 1932.

A third landscape that Clarice issued later in 1931 was not to sell so well. *Fantasque Mountain* has an orange and brown mountain, with a cottage and trees in front, and a yellow sky. The banding, generally blue, orange and green completes the design well. The lack of sales in 1931 makes it a rarity now, and it has become very collectable.

Gardenia was Clarice's most significant floral design in 1931 and was popular into 1932. Outlined in brown, it featured large salver-shaped flowers, with black and green leaves. When the main flower was orange the banding was yellow, when the flower was red, the banding was green, this colour combination proved attractive on a lot of Clarice's shapes.

Clarice introduced a new design in 1931 that was to be untypical of her output, but was ironically to remain in production until 1935. *Idyll* was a traditional design of a crinoline lady in a stylised garden, under a *Bizarre* tree. It was issued as part of the *Appliqué* range with heavy black and red banding, and proved popular.

Even more paintresses were recruited in 1931, among them Rene Dale. Rene's friendship with all the family, gives us an insight into Clarice's brothers and sisters, and her taste in interior decor.

"*Her brothers and sisters did not realise at the time the significance of her having her name on the ware. Dolly made the dresses for us when Nancy and I were bridesmaids. I stayed at the house one night, in the bedroom Clarice had painted with her sister Ethel. The ceiling was black with gold or silver stars, the furniture was all black with the drawers bright orange, and plain covers. Clarice liked to daub colour all over things that was how she was if she tried to paint ware, slap-dash, bang the paint on!*"

However, it was Rene Dale's scholarship and training at Burslem School of Art that

Bottom left:
Fruitburst
Bizarre
1930-1931
A motif of stylised fruit with orange lines radiating out from behind.
★★★★£££

Bottom right:
Full Circle
Bizarre
1933
A design of concentric black circles highlighted with green or yellow lines and spots.
★★★★£

Opposite:
Japan
Bizarre
1933-1934
A delicate pen outline of a tree with an oriental summerhouse behind. The sky and ground both in *Cafe-au-Lait*. Colourways blue and green.
★★★£££

Bottom:
Fruit
Fantasque
1929-1930
Geometric fruit and leaves in red, yellow, green and orange against a hatching of diagonal purple lines.
★★★★£££

Top:
Garland
Fantasque
1929
An early freehand design of stylised orange, yellow, blue and purple flowers, painted on a black ground, as a shoulder or rim decorations. Very similar to a design in the pattern books dated January 21st 1929, so this was probably one of the first floral designs after *Crocus*.
★★★££

Opposite:
Inspiration Knight Errant
1930-1931
A knight on horseback by a castle wall. Designed by John Butler as early as 1926. The outlining is probably by Ellen Brown.
★★★★££££
See also *Latona Knight Errant*.

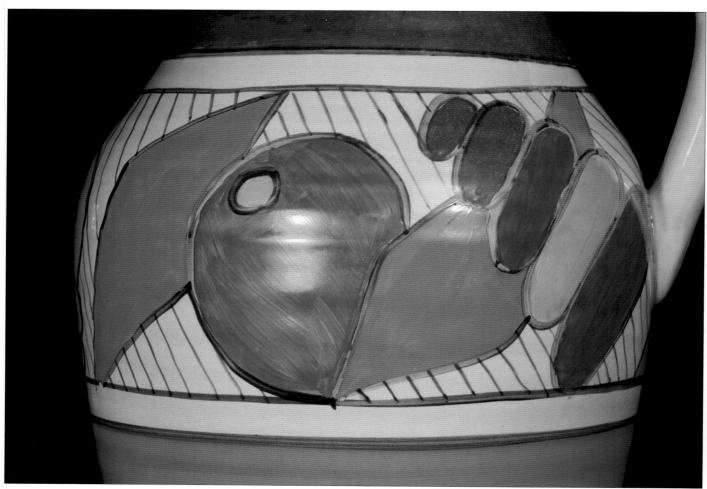

secured her an apprenticeship early in 1931. Rene remembers that for a while she and some of the younger girls used to avoid work by hiding in the old moulds shop at Newport. However, she soon started taking a pride in her work.

"*Clarice would come round to inspect what we had done, and if she didn't think it was good enough she would say so and tell us to rub it off and start again! When I got there the original Bizarre was going out and the designs with trees and cottages were coming in. Eventually I became an outliner, using a fine brush. Initially we used to copy from a water-colour but you would soon do it automatically - you did not look at the pattern. Sometimes you would change it gradually, and Clarice would come and make you go back to how it was originally done, which was of course how she would remember it.*"

Innovative designs, with new use of colours, that appeared in 1931 included *Tennis, Apples, Oranges & Lemons, Oranges* and *Farmhouse. Tennis* is a unique pattern as it broke the mould of Clarice's style at this time. Firstly it was painted completely freehand, rather than outlined and enamelled. It featured a startling colour combination including lilac, grey, blue and red, some examples were painted all-over the ware with no banding. When banding was added it was in red, purple and yellow. It is not surprising therefore, that it did not sell in great quantities in 1931, but is now highly collectable. It is an original design by Clarice that does not really fall into the cubist style, but is also not Art Deco.

Apples initially appears to be a simple, balanced pattern, but is more sophisticated on closer inspection. Although the apples are naturally coloured in two shades of green blended together, the leaves are in combinations of orange, yellow, lilac and pink. On good examples, the banding makes the pieces vibrate.

The black, orange and red fruit, and black leaves of *Oranges & Lemons* makes it a very strident design, it was probably superceded later in the year with the lighter shades of *Oranges*. This was a simpler design of panels of the fruit with mauve, blue and green leaves and orange banding.

This page:
Geometric Flowers
Fantasque
1929
Cubist flowers on black stems, in early *Bizarre* colours with rust red banding and detail.
★★★★★£££££

Opposite:
Latona Dahlia
Latona
1930-1931
Linear and curved lines, with blue, pink and lilac flowers and green leaves.
An orange colourway also known.
★★★★£££££

Farmhouse was one of the first landscapes with which Clarice moved towards more natural colours. Its brown, rust and green scene proved popular, being in production until at least 1933, an example dated 1935 is also known.

As sales of *Inspiration* declined, the technique was adapted for use in some new ranges. *Marigold* featured an *Inspiration* background with the outlines of the flowers left clear; these were then applied in enamels on the glaze. *Clouvre* used a similar process on a darker ground, with multi-coloured flowers. Neither range sold in large quantities, but ware in stock was sold for some time afterwards. An attempt was made to revive the *Inspiration* technique with *Opalesque* ware in 1934.

Clarice issued a mass of innovative fancies in 1931, one of which revealed surprising influences. Her shape 463, a combined *Cigarette & Match Holder*, which consisted of two semi-circular containers back to back, is similar to a shape made in 1905 by Josef Hoffmann for the Wiener Werkstätte. It is remarkable that Clarice was aware of such work in 1931, but it demonstrates her extensive interest in design. The shape 463 was just one of many smoker's accoutrements. Apart from ashtrays in various shapes, she made her very British *Lido Lady* ashtray (shape 561). This was made in two sizes and the lady wore a cloche hat, fashionable trousers known as beach pyjamas, and held a towel. A neat *Smokers set* (shape 467) consisted of a box, with four small individual ashtrays all on a tray, and shape 420 was a *Cigarette holder & ashtray*.

One of the most popular pieces in Clarice's *Conical* range was issued in August 1931. The actual use of a pure cone shape as a sugar dredger did not happen until this time even though the concept had been used in June 1929 for her shape 378 and 379 vases. The *Conical Sugar Dredger* proved an ideal shape for her designs and a popular addition to the Thirties breakfast table. It has also become one of the most popular additions to a collection today.

Clarice introduced new designs for her *Appliqué* range during late 1931 which were only briefly produced. *Etna*, a landscape with a volcano and coast scene, *Monsoon*, a tropical scene, only known to date on a plaque found in South Africa. Clarice revived

This page:
Honeydew
Bizarre and Clarice Cliff
1935 onwards
Etched flowers in green and yellow similar to *Rhodanthe*, painted centrally on tea and tableware. Also a version with pink and blue flowers.
Sold mainly to retailers in the south-west of England.
★£
See also *Sundew*.

Opposite:
Latona Bouquet
Latona
1930
Pendant petunia shaped flowers with blue and green leaves.
★★★★£££

Opposite:
Latona Flowerheads
Latona
1929
Stylised flower heads in *Appliqué* yellow, blue and orange, above rough vertical blue stripes.
★★★★£££

Opposite:
Latona Mushroom
Latona
1929
Stylised mushrooms outlined in green with lilac, blue, orange and red colours.
★★★★★£££

Opposite:
Latona Red Roses
Latona
1930-1931 (matchings to 1935)
Stylised roses and black leaves covering all the ware, painted in the style of a stencil.
★★★£££

Opposite:
Latona Thistle
Latona
1929-1930
A geometric thistle head in red and black.
★★★★★£££

Opposite:
Latona Tree
Latona
1929-1930
A tree with a black trunk, and pendulous foliage in red, orange, green and blue.
★★★★£££

This page:
Sundew
Bizarre and Clarice Cliff
1936
Flowers in the *Rhodanthe* style, but in pink and green.
★£
See also *Honeydew*.

Top:
Gloria
Bizarre
1930-1931
A range produced with underglaze decoration in thin water-colours, covered with a creamy *Latona* style glaze. Designs are simplified versions of other *Bizarre* patterns and include *Crocus, Tulip* and *Bridge*.
★★★★£££

Bottom left:
Hollyhocks
Bizarre
1936-1937
Freehand flowers in lilac and pink with beige and yellow detail. Also pattern number 6741.
★★£

Bottom right:
Hollyrose
Bizarre
1932
Stylised flowers in pink, brown and yellow, with blue contour line effect between.
★★★★★££

Opposite:
Kew
Fantasque
1932-1933
A red pagoda between wedge and bubble shape trees similar to *Trees & House*, with a bridge and poplar trees on reverse. Produced as both a full design, and on tableware in a cartouche.
Full design ★★★★££££
Cartouche ★★★★££

the first two *Appliqué* designs, *Lugano* and *Lucerne* briefly in late 1931. These later examples were only issued in the blue colourway. They can be distinguished as they have slightly thinner colours, and a printed *Appliqué* mark rather than a hand-painted one. However, as with all of Clarice's designs it is dangerous to assume a final date of production - the last piece of *Appliqué Lucerne* is known to date from November 1933.

Another significant part of the Clarice Cliff story developed in September 1931. The *Bizooka*, the pottery horse that had started as a drawing in 1929 became a reality. Colley Shorter was probably behind this piece of pure promotional genius, turning the drawing into a real pottery horse. The *Bizooka* frame was made of steel rods, and was easily assembled and dismantled. The pottery was pre-drilled before it was fired with holes in appropriate positions, then assembled on the frame with felt pads between each piece to stop breakages. The shapes and designs used to produce the real *Bizooka* were very different to the earlier drawing. The head was two plaques, with two bowls for the mouth, the neck was vases and the body was an umbrella stand, all in Clarice's latest designs.

The *Bizooka* was a runaway success! It was the centrepiece of the Newport Pottery float for the 1931 Crazy Day parade. This was to raise funds for local hospitals, and the theme was "Help your Hospital, Save The Race". The girls dressed up as jockeys and ran alongside the lorry. Standing nearly six foot tall with candles in its shape 331 candlestick ears, the *Bizooka* was so impressive that it overshadowed some other promotional devices Clarice dreamt up at this time. A small *Bizarre* man had candlesticks for legs, sabots for feet, a double-handled *Lotus* jug for his body and arms, and a shape 370 globe head. He was pulling the *Bizooka* on the float.

Clarice also dreamt up a *Bizarre* tree. Onto the cut-out shape of a tree were hung "fruit" - a selection of small plates in Clarice's designs, including *Melon, Umbrellas, Football, Circle Tree, Sunray* and *Swirls*. This may have been made before the *Bizooka* but it certainly appeared alongside it in window displays. The tree was over five feet high so its impact must have been immense.

This page:
Hydrangea
Bizarre
1934-1935
Delicately drawn flowers, with fine bands and lines over the top. Colourways are orange or green.
★★££

Opposite:
Lightning
Bizarre
1929-1930
A blue and purple disc crossed with a black flash, with red, orange and yellow geometric shapes above and below.
★★★★£££££

In September 1931 the *Bizooka* was exhibited at the First Avenue Hotel in Holborn, where it was photographed with well-known personalities. These included Jack Hilton the band leader and Sir Malcolm Campbell, who was a national hero as in February he had set a world land-speed record of 246 mph at Daytona Beach, Florida, and had been knighted upon his return. His presence at the exhibition was the British equivalent of having Rudolph Valentino and Clark Gable endorse *Bizarre*. This may explain the untypically nervous look on Colley Shorter's face in the photograph of him with Campbell inspecting a *Bizarre* plate, as the *Bizooka* ignores them both.

The annual show at the First Avenue Hotel was a key London trade show where the company would get many of its orders for Christmas stock. Every account was sent an invitation, together with an up to date coloured leaflet showing new designs. Clarice showed her *Conical* sugar dredgers, which became very popular, smoker's sets, her *Lido Lady* ashtray and *Cock-a-doodle-doo* cruet sets. The displays secured orders from America, Germany and Holland, again attracting coverage in national newspapers.

Clarice excelled herself again in 1931 with some innovative vase shapes. Her *Flower Tube* vases featured two thin tubes with a flat 'S' shaped fin in-between. These vases were similar, except for the fact that the shape 464 had a foot, but the shape 465 did not. However, they again stretched the ability of the mould makers, as the tubes had to be cast separately to the fin and then attached, when fired many examples suffered stress cracks. This kept production of these shapes low, as did the retail price of eighteen shillings and sixpence.

As interest in *Bizarre* grew, Clarice was interviewed extensively about her work. One article in the *Bristol Times* was by Millicent Hardman, the grooming from Colley Shorter, and success of her ideas, had given her a great deal more confidence.

"I have always loved bright colours, and think the modern idea of using these for pottery and china adds such a cheerful note to our tables and to our rooms. The more or less stereotyped and tame designs that preceded them were, after all, rather drab, and lacking in interest. I love mixed bold tints - rich oranges, reds, greens, blues and mauves. These make a glorious riot of colour on large articles of pottery. On breakfast and dinner sets though, too much design is not effective, but harmony of colours is most important."

Perhaps the most interesting aspect of the article however, is that Clarice comes across as very aware of industrial design. She explains how she linked her design ideas to functionality and price, and the needs of women.

"I know that women today like to strike an individual note in their homes, so it has been my aim to devise pottery that will help them to realise their ideal. I am aware that in these times of money scarcity, articles that have a useful as well as decorative purpose have a more general appeal. Labour saving is another important factor I have taken into consideration. Consequently I am showing this year several things made in pottery for which this medium has never been used before. Also you will notice my table china is designed on lines that simplify its cleaning. There are no corners or fluting to harbour dust and grease and the handles are of a sensible shape that makes the articles easy to move about."

Clarice's confidence is shown by the continued use of the first person throughout the interview, she never alluded to, "we". Colley Shorter's realisation that linking a product with a real person gave a unique selling point, came decades before "designer products". The use of Clarice as a figurehead at this time and a promotable personality, was something virtually unheard of in the Potteries in the Thirties.

More publicity for *Bizarre* appeared in the press. *The Daily Sketch* newspaper carried a story about the introduction of a radio in the *Bizarre* shop. This was probably initially done to discourage the *Bizarre* girls chatting as they worked, but it was soon realised that it had the effect of speeding up the decorating process! Never one to miss a promotional opportunity, Colley Shorter drew this to the attention of the paper which included a photograph of a selection of paintresses decorating around the wireless.

Opposite:
Persian (Inspiration)
1930-1931
A range of Isnic style patterns produced in the *Inspiration* glaze technique, in pinks, mauves and blues.
★★★£££££

Bottom right:
Goldstone
Bizarre
1933-1934
A range of ware using a speckled earth-coloured clay for the body, covered in clear shiny glaze. Numerous unclassified simple freehand designs: primarily seen on vases, *Lynton* tea and coffeesets but also face masks and some other fancies.
★★£

Top:
Industry
Latona
1929-1930
An industrial motif of symbols for water, electricity and power, all hand-painted on a *Latona* glaze plate. Two identical examples known. Designed and perhaps painted by an industrial apprentice at Newport Pottery, Ron Birks, who also designed the *Grotesque* face mask illustrated on page 1.

Bottom left:
Kandina
Fantasque
1929
A stylised tree with an amoebic shape either side, under a border of 'V' shapes.
★★★★★£££££

Opposite:
Line Jazz
Bizarre
1930-1931
Straight and 'L' shaped lines in blue and black among cubist shapes in orange, brown and yellow.
★★★★★£££££

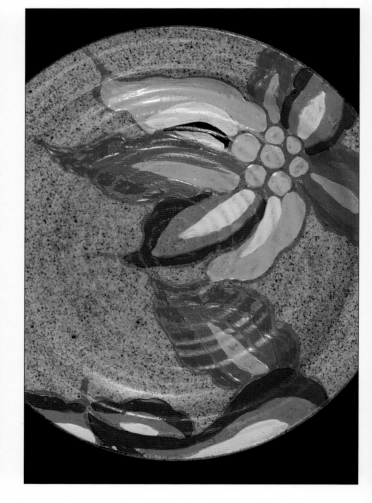

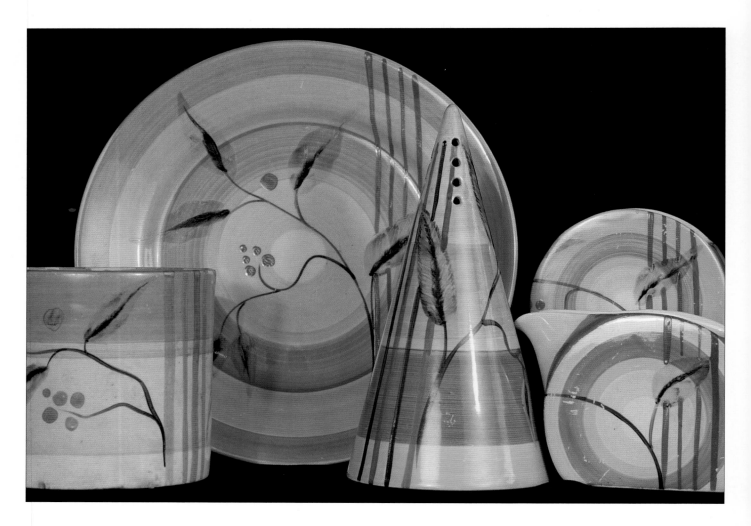

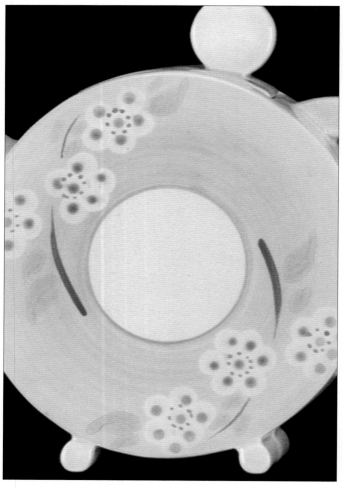

"*Working to music has increased output by twenty-five percent at least, in the hand-painting department at Newport Pottery Works. The introduction of the music was suggested by the girls. Instead of taking their minds off work, jazz tunes and classical melodies assist them to concentrate.*"

Daffodil, a new shape of tea and coffee ware, was named after the curves of the body, and the embossed linear forms on the handles which resembled the flower. The range was complete having its own cups, milk and sugar. However, it did not follow the previous *Conical* and *Stamford* shapes, its graceful styling owed more to Art Nouveau. Clarice seems to have done this intentionally, because although it is found in some landscape designs, it was initially combined with a new style of earthenware body called *Damask Rose*.

Damask Rose was made by casting the ware with slip mixed with a pink colourant. To achieve this very advanced finish it was necessary to re-open the Newport Pottery slip house where the slip maker Albert Simpson mixed the colourant with the standard slip used at Wilkinson's. This had to be done in a separate area or the colourant would inevitably have got into Wilkinson's earthenware. Once cast and fired the biscuit ware pieces were then given a clear glaze. This was a very advanced quality of body and finish for this time, equal to any of the ware being produced at Wedgwood. Sensibly Clarice used this soft toning colour for tableware. To allow the effect to show through it was decorated just with small fruit or floral motifs, painted freehand. *Damask Rose* was enthusiastically received in the papers at the time, both the glaze and shape were praised, but it was only produced for about a year.

During 1931 new landscape designs appeared that were issued well into 1932. *Red Roofs* featured a typical Clarice cottage with a flowering climbing plant against it. A fence led to a huge orange flower that was the reverse of the design. *House & Bridge* had a sharp palette of red, orange, yellow and brown with black lining. It was in regular production for at least a year, and examples are known from 1934, but it was never offered in another colourway which is puzzling as it was a popular pattern. Many examples of this design were outlined by Ellen Browne, and some bear a "B" mark hand-painted on the base, which tend to confirm this. Forty-four years later when the first book was written about Clarice Cliff *House & Bridge* was featured on the cover, and until its original name was re-discovered collectors referred to it as *Front Cover*.

These classic Clarice Cliff designs appeared at a time when Britain was literally in crisis. Salaries of teachers, civil servants and many others had been cut by fifteen percent, and unemployment was nearly three million.

The staff in the *Bizarre* shop were oblivious to much of the reality of 1931. They were after all still young, and occasionally when Clarice and Colley were away things would get riotous. Outliner Fred Salmon found a mouse frozen in a bowl of water and chased Mary Brown around the *Bizarre* shop with it, intending to drop it down her back. Despite this he was very popular with the girls, and sometimes entertained them by swinging across the canal on the crane used to unload the barges. Inevitably his bravado led to an accident and they watched in horror as he plunged into the Trent-Mersey canal. Fred saved himself, but despite hiding in the saggar warehouse where he dried his clothes, his absence from the shop was noticed that afternoon and he had some of his pay docked.

Gibraltar marked a major new style for Clarice. Forsaking the strong orange that *Bizarre* had been founded on, she used a combination of pink, mauve, blue, yellow and a little green - for the first time Clarice restricted herself to pastel shades. Some of these colours were more expensive than the standard *Bizarre* ones, and perhaps for this reason the attractive Harrison's Pink that was a key part of the palette was not used extensively. *Gibraltar* was outlined in purple, and featured the rock and some white-sailed yachts on a blue sea. Some examples even had small dots to represent sailors in the boat.

Kathy Keeling, the paintress who did the sample pieces, soon found herself extremely busy outlining. During the fifteen months it was produced she was assisted by other outliners. Its success was partly because small fancies decorated in the design, such as

Bottom left:
Honiton
Clarice Cliff
1936-1937
Shaded banding with flower petals formed by dabbing the little finger in the wet surface and then painting detail in.
This was originated by Bizarre girl Marjory Higginson.
★★★££

Bottom right:
Islands
Bizarre
1936
A small central print of a stylised island with hand-painted banding, green and blue colourways.
★★★★★£

Top:
Kelverne
Clarice Cliff
1936
Horizontal shading with freehand foliage and berries. Colourways brown, blue and yellow.
Referred to as Grey Leaves in Collecting Clarice Cliff.
★★★££

coasters, sabots and ashtrays, were popular at shops at seaside towns as a momento of a holiday week on the coast.

Clarice issued another new style during 1931 called *Cafe-au-Lait*. The name referred to a process where the ware was covered all over in colour with a special stippling brush. Designs such as *Autumn*, *Bobbins*, or *Oranges* would then be executed over the *Cafe-au-Lait* ground. It is a confusing name as the effect was produced in green, blue and yellow as well as the brown it implied. *Cafe-au-Lait* seems to have been issued for some time, and even merited its own backstamp.

The year ended with yet more publicity for *Bizarre*. The girls were excited as the entire shop was to be photographed, they all did their hair and wore make-up. The photo spread covered the whole back page of the *Daily Sketch* on December 4th. Captioned "Girl artists working on *Bizarre* pottery", in the front row were Phyllis Woodhead, Winnie Pound, Gerty Love and Lily Barrow. Promotionally the headline above this was a dream come true: "How famous *Bizarre* ware is made at Stoke."

Other pictures showed warehouse staff taking ware from the saggars arriving from the ovens, and paintresses enamelling. Two girl assistants wearing their best pleated skirts posed by a display of ware in the showroom. The picture was captioned, "Some examples of *Inspiration* ware designed by Miss Clarice Cliff, the only woman Art Director in the Potteries."

To optimise this promotional opportunity Colley Shorter purchased 1000 copies of the *Daily Sketch* and made sure they were mailed to every outlet in the United Kingdom. Less than four years after the launch of *Bizarre* Clarice had reached the pinnacle of her career, and forever changed the male-dominated world of the Potteries.

Opposite and page 129:
Lucerne
Appliqué
1930-1931 (matchings to 1933)
A castle in a mountainous landscape of fir trees, the colour of the sky indicates colourways, blue or orange.
Partly based on a pochoir print by Edouard Benedictus.
Colourways:
Blue ★★★★★££££
Orange ★★★★★£££££

This page:
Colley Shorter's ideal headline shown on the back cover of the Daily Sketch dated December 4 1931.

Top:
Lily
Fantasque
1929-1930
A brashly drawn lily and leaves. The orange colourway was originally numbered as *Fantasque* 104, Lily Brown as *Fantasque* 107.
A rare colourway known from two examples, has the leaves painted orange, the flower left honeyglaze, the background black.
★★★££

Bottom:
Lisbon
Bizarre
1931
Perhaps an adaptation of the earlier *Arabesque* design; overlapping squares with floral motifs, and a border of curvilinear style on a *Cafe-au-Lait* ground.
★★★★££

Opposite:
Lucerne
See page 126.

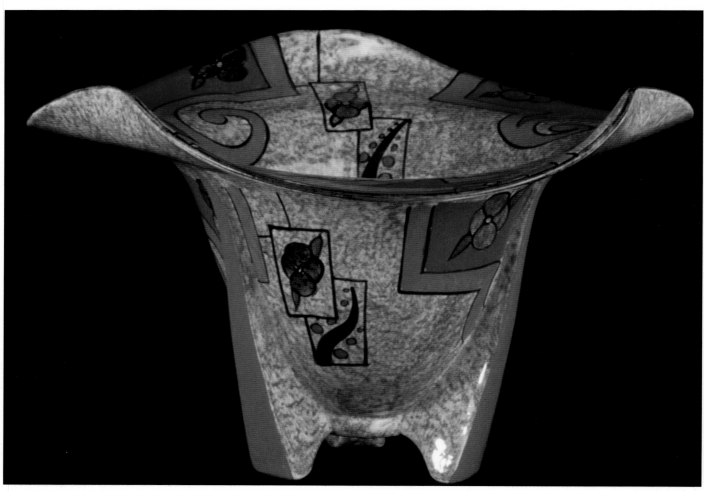

CHAPTER 6

1932
CRUISING ALONG

Clarice Cliff and Colley Shorter were to breeze through 1932 although the financial crisis in Britain was at its worse that year. Having brought about a revolution in the shape and design of tableware, fancies and art pottery during the depression, they were able to weather the storm. Many potbanks that had clung to more ordinary ware closed down, but Clarice and Colley were now able to consolidate their position.

The year again saw a large display of *Bizarre* and *Fantasque* at the British Industries Fair, which Clarice supervised with the aid of Hilda Lovatt and a team of factory workers. Her displays were more sophisticated now, more preparation enabled Clarice to concentrate on them. The publicity shots for *Bizarre* also changed. Clarice had taken these since 1928, but as she got busier this was a job she reluctantly relinquished. A London photographer, Elsie F. Collins, took over in 1932 and the promotional shots sent out by the factory were more proficient and correctly-lit, but lacked the style of Clarice's. However, she retained a life-long interest in photography, which was also one of Colley Shorter's hobbies.

During 1932 some staff left. Fred Salmon recalled, "Clarice was doing ultra modern stuff - I was more interested in the art side with flowers." He joined the nearby Burgess & Leigh factory, and later went to Royal Doulton as a figure painter. Clarice's first paintress, Gladys Scarlett, also left. The other girls remember that Gladys had a volatile personality and used to mimic Clarice. On one occasion she walked up and down the shop swinging a coat belt behind her, imitating Clarice's walk and long hair,

This page:
London
Bizarre
1930-1931
An abstract design of a red crescent with orange, yellow, green and blue geometric forms crossing it, between thick brown banding, and thin red lines.
★★★★★££££

Opposite and page 133:
Lugano
Appliqué
1930-1931
A waterwheel in a mountainous landscape, the colour of the sky indicates the colourways of blue or orange.
★★★★££££££

much to the amusement of the girls. Clarice entered whilst she was doing this, but for whatever reason turned round without saying anything.

Gladys had been given wage rises but felt she was worth more, and left for a better-paid job at John Stevenson's Royal Pottery in Burslem. She briefly achieved the status of designer and a few plates are known with an elaborate printed backstamp *Royal Venton Ware Handcraft by Gladys Scarlett*, but the designs are indifferent floral ones. The project clearly suffered from the effect of the depression as Gladys left quite quickly, and the factory changed to making tiles.

Harold Walker and John Shaw had been promised when they joined that they would be allowed to design. However, apart from one written reference to a landscape by Harold Walker in the Newport Pottery pattern books, they were never credited on the ware itself for any designing they may have done. However, a design called *Car & Skyscraper*, found on an *Isis* vase, is identical to a water-colour drawing from Harold Walker's Burslem School of Art exercise books. The vase lacks a backstamp, it is believed to be just a sample.

Despite the depression that was seriously affecting the country, business remained good in 1932 so new staff were bought in to be trained by Lily Slater in the hand-painting techniques of the *Bizarre* shop. New girls included Ivy Tunicliff, Lily Dabbs and outliner Ellen Browne's sister Mollie, who joined as a bander and liner. Mollie's memories show that Clarice had since her early days become much more formal with her staff.

"*We had to clock in and she would stand where nobody could see her and watch to see who was late. If you were frequently late you were sent home for the day. Clarice was very strict but it was good discipline. She came round at about 9.45 to see how we were all working. She hardly ever spoke to us, she was very aloof.*"

New ranges that appeared in 1932 included the floral patterns *Nasturtium*, *Chintz*, *Cowslip* and *Canterbury Bells* and landscapes included *Orange Roof Cottage*, *Limberlost*,

Bottom left:
Feather & Leaves
Fantasque
1929-1930
An orange stylised feather shape, against a yellow and green geometric background, with a simple stem and three black leaves.
★★★★£££

Bottom right:
Keyhole
Bizarre
1929
A geometric design in yellow and orange, sometimes with green.
★★★★£££

Opposite:
Lugano
See page 130.

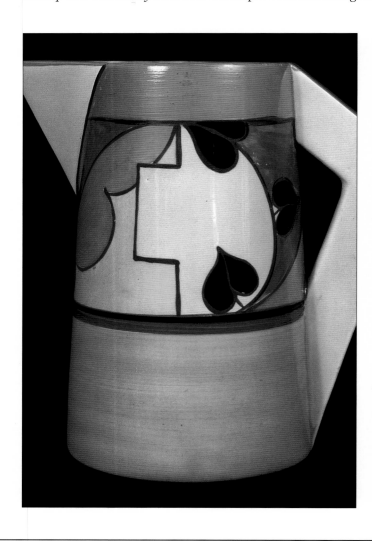

and *Poplar*. Each of these brought in some new element to the landscape that she had not previously used. Her imagination with these seemed to run riot.

The promotion of *Bizarre* was always a priority with both Clarice and Colley and another method they used was to issue advertising ware painted with *Clarice Cliff* or *Bizarre* logos. This was done in *Inspiration* style in the early Thirties, and a *Conical* bowl just with the names and banding is also known. The most imaginative was probably one where the word *Bizarre* was growing out of the foliage of the *Limberlost* tree. Such pieces were probably used both for exhibitions and as promotional devices in stores.

Clarice's fascination with texture and natural effects on her ware continued, and she issued *Marguerite* a large range of teaware and fancies on which modelled flowers formed the handles or knobs, the bodies were stippled in *Cafe-au-Lait* in a choice of colours.

The *Delecia* name was revived for a design of orange and lemon fruit with grey, green and yellow runnings underneath which Clarice called *Delecia Citrus*. Elsie Nixon, Winnie Davis and Nora Dabbs decorated this and it sold well for nearly two years. A little later *Delecia Pansies* also appeared, strangely with *Nasturtium* style flowers. These were in blue, pink, mauve and yellow, with amber, green and brown runnings. *Delecia Pansies* proved popular and examples from as late as 1935 are known.

The more pleasant side to the girl's work was that in the summer their hand-painting demonstrations were in busy seaside towns. Elsie Nixon and Marjory Higginson went to Haven's in Westcliff-on-Sea, where they had time to relax on the coast in the sunshine.

The *Bizooka* continued to be used by the factory to publicise *Bizarre*, and the 1932 Crazy Day float was "Kindle a Kandle for the Kiddies Kamp", raising money for a children's convalescent home in Rhyll in Wales. The *Bizooka* fitted the theme as its ears were candlesticks with candles in.

Bottom right:
Le Bon Dieu
1932-1933
A range of shapes modelled to resemble tree trunks or boles; initially these were decorated in brown and green runnings to resemble moss and bark, and each was marked on the base "I think that I shall never see a form as lovely as a tree".
When the range failed to sell, the shapes were then issued in designs such as Nasturtium.
★★★£

Bottom left:
Lorna
Clarice Cliff
1936
A landscape in natural colours of a cottage, a bridge, and a river flowing into the foreground, with some red and orange bushes behind the cottage.
★★★££

Opposite:
Luxor
Bizarre
1929-1930
Landscape with pyramids on the horizon, and stylised trees in the foreground. Colourways named after the colour of the sky, orange or blue.
★★★★££££

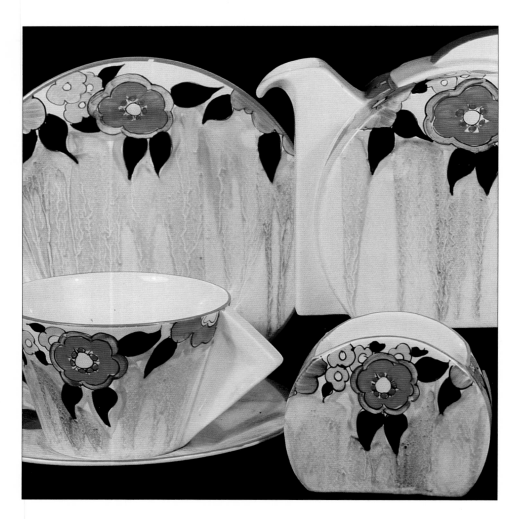

Bottom left:
Killarney
Bizarre
1935
A geometric design, very similar to the
Original Bizarre but produced in pastel
green and brown.
★★★££
See also *Sungold*.

Bottom right:
Leaf Tree
Bizarre
1933
A black tree trunk with giant orange leaves
on green ground with a row of stylised
flowers.
★★★★★£££

Top:
Lydiat
Bizarre
1933
Orange and brown or green and yellow
flowers in black outline with amber
runnings underneath.
★★££

Opposite:
Marigold
Bizarre
1931
On glaze decoration of marigolds in
orange and yellow, on underglaze blue
Inspiration style ground.
★★★★££££

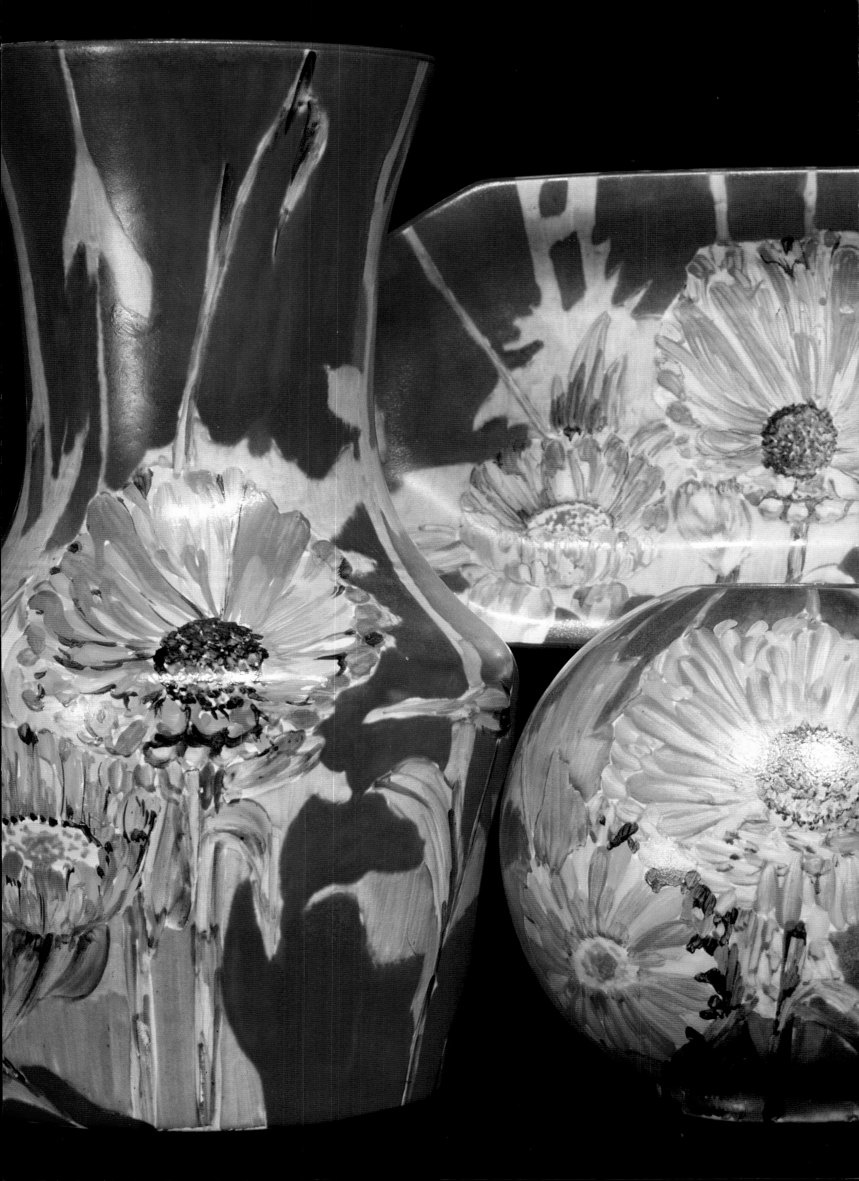

The factory made two *Bizookas* and lent them to stockists to publicise the ware. The ceramic horse was also featured in a press-release, accompanied by a picture of Clarice, which was published around the world! The *Pasadena Evening Post* said, "Miss Cliff has often been criticised for what they call low comedy, but she laughs at their well meant advice and reminds them that her business has increased steadily in the few years she has employed her talents for herself." Clarice was then quoted:

"*Having a little fun at my work does not make me any less of an artist, and people who appreciate truly beautiful and original creations in pottery are not frightened by innocent tomfoolery!*"

The *Bizarre* girls went on yet more demonstrations: Mary Brown, Elsie Nixon and Ellen Browne went to Lance & Lance at Weston-Super-Mare in Somerset, Spooner's in Plymouth, and Pauldon's in Manchester.

One *Bizarre* Girl who was not to make it through 1932 was Kitty Oakes. She applied the dark blue on an order of *Blue Chintz* too thickly and it blistered in the glost kiln. Clarice took it to show her and sacked her. She was not normally so severe, but the girls recall that Clarice could be quite officious, and made a rule that they had to clock-in with their overalls on when they arrived at 8am. Some girls got lax about this rule and one day Clarice waited behind a door for them to enter and caught them all out.

Clarice's most adventurous line in 1932 was created in August. The story of *Le Bon Dieu* is yet another part of the Clarice Cliff mystique.

"*One day a friend gave me a polished wooden block, part of a tree trunk of unusual shape. The moment I saw this the idea came to me to create pottery, taking actual tree trunks as my models.*"

Reverting to her natural fascination with modelling, Clarice threw herself into making the natural, distorted shapes that were like tree boles. These were decorated in running browns and greens to simulate bark and tree moss. Her confidence in the

Bottom left:
Liberty
Bizarre
1929-1930
The name given to ware simply covered all over in bands of random width and colour, which the girls produced to bulk-up orders, as it was easy to decorate.
★£

Bottom right:
Lodore
Bizarre
1929
A print outline with flowers in green and yellow, and black hatching.
★★★★££

Opposite:
May Avenue
Fantasque
1933
An avenue of red-roofed houses and spade-shaped trees, with a tree in green *Cafe-au-Lait* foliage, all in pen outline.
Based on an oil painting "Landscape at Cagnes" by Modigliani.
★★★★£££££

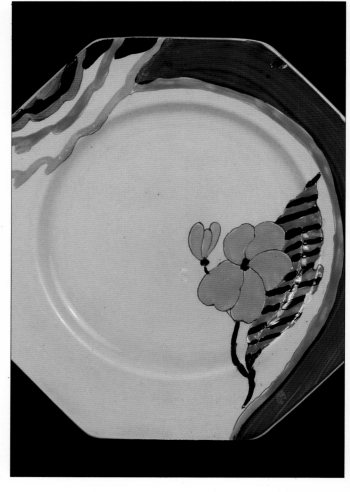

Bottom:
Marguerite
Bizarre
1932-1933
A range with embossed flowers forming the handles or a motif on ware with body stippled in *Cafe-au-Lait*.
★★£

Top:
Melon (Picasso Fruit)
See page 142.

Opposite:
Mountain
Fantasque
1931-1932
A stylised tree and cottage in the foreground with a mountain rising behind.
Colourways:
Orange ★★★★£££££
Pastel ★★★★★£££££

ware was clear as she made a large range of bowls, vases, a complete teaset, a biscuit barrel and jampot, including shape numbers 589, 560, 562 and 573 to 577.

Colley Shorter believed in *Le Bon Dieu* and with Clarice he drew up an extensive publicity launch. Greta Lane the wife of a Shorter & Sons salesman was recruited especially to tour outlets to sell the ware. When after six months it was clear it was not going to sell, the remaining stock of shapes were then treated the same way as the failed *Archaic* range and issued in other designs such as *Nasturtium*. The most fascinating thing about the ware is the story of its genesis, and the fact that on the base of each piece was the quotation, "I think that I shall never see a form as lovely as a tree."

Patina was another innovative style Clarice introduced in 1932. Like *Le Bon Dieu* it involved use of texture on ware to create an unusual finish, but it was more akin to the spirit of *Bizarre* as it used existing shapes. Before glazing, pieces were covered in random splashes of slip that had been given a pale grey or pink colouring to make them stand out against the body. The ware was then honeyglazed and decorated in new freehand designs. It was difficult for the paintresses to outline because of the encrusted surface so initially these designs were freehand and included *Patina Coastal*, *Tree* and *Country*. Subsequently, standard designs were used on the ware - examples in *Rhodanthe*, *Blue Firs* and *Secrets* are known.

The factory staged another show at the First Avenue Hotel, London in September 1932. Colley Shorter hired personalities to promote the ware; Marie Tempest, Marion Lorne, Adrienne Allen, Christopher Stone and Leslie Henson were amongst those appearing. They were photographed with Clarice and Colley. One picture shows Colley Shorter taking tea with the actresses out of *Daffodil* shape cups.

Christopher Stone was one of the first presenters on the new *British Broadcasting Company*, which was still a novelty in 1932. An amusing photograph showed Stone threatening to drown a *Teddy Bear* bookend in a glass tank in which live goldfish were swimming around some of Clarice's *Tree* figures. Other parts of Clarice's earthenware

Pages 140, 142, 143:
Melon (Picasso Fruit)
Fantasque
1930-1931
A band of overlapping, geometric fruit, with contour line effect between. Most commonly with dominant orange, but also produced in colourways of red, green, blue and pastel.
Colourways:
Orange ★★★£££££
Pastel ★★★★£££££
Red ★★★★★£££££
Green ★★★★£££££
Blue ★★★★★£££££

menagerie included *Elephant* napkin-rings, and a *Chick cocoa pot*. Clarice and Colley were probably the first people to hire a D J to publicise pottery.

Another of Colley Shorter's innovations was that apart from paying personalities to endorse ware at exhibitions he managed to obtain coverage afterwards in women's magazines, which had a large circulation in the Thirties. *Modern Home* carried a picture story about Marion Lorne following her appearance at the First Avenue Hotel.

"*Miss Marion Lorne who in her own inimitable way has delighted thousands of playgoers by her acting in 'Roadhouse' at the Whitehall Theatre, takes a great interest in her home and loves to go out in search of pretty accessories to add to the charm of her rooms. She chose this lovely fruit set she said because it was so gay - not strikingly modern but just beautifully coloured. The set consists of six plates and a fruit bowl designed specifically for Miss Lorne by Clarice Cliff . The ground is cream with a design of orange and yellow citrus fruit , and leaves of smoky blue and light and dark green, outlined in a soft shade of brown. Although she is a home lover Marion is a thoroughly outdoor sort of person and every Saturday she and her playwright husband Walter Hackett motor down to their bungalow in Sussex. Even when she is in London Marion never missed her daily walk, she and Ambrose her dog set out solemnly to do their regulation mile and a half. But don't expect to meet them in the streets, you must look upwards if you want to see them for their route is always the same, up and down the balcony of the flat overlooking Piccadilly!*"

When Clarice returned from such shows her excitement about who she had met led to informal interludes with her girls. She would tell them about the stars of stage and radio she had met, and produced large autographed photographs of them. These moments were brief, however, as the competition for her ware was such that stockists were now demanding exclusive designs.

Clarice now had the confidence to adapt her own work for new designs. An example

Opposite:
Mondrian
Bizarre
1929-1930
An abstract design of overlapping squares mainly in orange, blue, black and yellow although there are some variations known. On a vase or bowl the design repeats and wraps around the vessel.
Although named by collectors after the abstract painter Piet Mondrian, the design is not really typical of his work but closer to that of his friend, the architect and furniture designer Gerrit Rietveld. Rietveld's classic 1918 Red/Blue Chair was originally produced in plain wood until at Mondrian's suggestion Rietveld coloured it in a similar style to the experimental paintings which later became Mondrian's trademark.
★★★★££££

This page:
Oasis
Bizarre
1933
A landscape with a large blue and pink cloud shaped tree, with yellow tufted grass in front.
★★★★£££

is *Kew* which appeared in September 1932. She took elements from the bubble tree and fir tree from *Trees & House*, added a further tree, a bridge and a pagoda, naming the new design after Kew Gardens near London. However, a new refinement was coming into her work. Although she loved all-over designs, there was a growing demand for more delicate tableware; *Kew* was issued in both these forms right from its launch. For tableware the motif was delicately hand-painted as a cartouche on the edge of plates and tureens, whereas vases and lampbases had the design full size.

Kew was one of the many new lines launched at "Modern Tableware by Clarice Cliff", an exhibition at Barker's store in London from the 24th October 1932. Clarice personally arranged thirty table-settings, and the literature from the exhibition said, "To see this modern display of china and table settings is to take a mental leap into the future." Clarice co-ordinated her tableware with matching cloths and napkins embroidered in the same designs, and even lampshades were decorated to match. She worked hard appearing at the exhibition every day. It is difficult to estimate the impact of this exhibition but there are many examples of *Kew* on tableware so it must have stimulated sales, and certainly no one else in the Potteries was using such personality-led events to publicise their ware.

Writers on the Potteries have retrospectively attempted to compare Susie Cooper's achievements with Clarice Cliff's. The historical context is that in 1930 Susie Cooper had ten hand-paintresses whereas Clarice Cliff had over sixty. These authors overlook the fact that by 1932 Clarice had produced a hundred shapes, over two hundred hand-painted designs and received extensive publicity for *Bizarre*. They also ignore the differences in their techniques. Susie Cooper's ware was nearly always painted freehand, the majority of Clarice's was outlined, enamelled and then banded, which achieved an entirely different effect. Susie Cooper's designs were certainly stylish, but they never captured the charisma and colour of Clarice Cliff's work.

The recognition Susie Cooper was to enjoy began in 1932, when she had her first stand at the *British Industries Fair*. Until then her hand-painted ware using blanks

Opposite:
Monsoon
Appliqué
1931
A yellow and green tree, with black trunk on a yellow and purple striped ground against an orange sky, to its left giant purple flowers rush from the ground, to the right, a green and blue hill capped by an ornamental arch.
Known from one example.
★★★★★£££££

This page:
Moonflower
Bizarre
1933
A green flower outlined in yellow with oblongs in grey, green, yellow and brown, there is also a rarer blue colourway.
★★★££

from other factories was certainly not as celebrated, successful or abundant as *Bizarre*. Clarice Cliff had been selling *Bizarre* almost world wide for six years when exports of Susie Cooper ware started from March 1933. Susie Cooper's first innovative shape, the *Kestrel*, was launched at the British Industries Fair in 1932, by which time Clarice was firmly established. The vogue Clarice had created for tableware and fancies designed by a woman for women, paved the way for other women to follow in her footsteps.

At the end of 1932 change was in the air in the form of a project given momentum by the Prince of Wales. In a speech he had stated that "British Industry must raise the standard of design in its products for in design it is outstripped by other countries." This co-incided with the publication of the Gorell committee's Report on Art and Education, which recommended a closer link between top artists and manufacturing companies. The project was to culminate in exhibitions of the results of the collaboration.

In the Potteries the local branch of the Society of Industrial Artists steered by Gordon Forsyth drew up a list of artists who would be commissioned to contribute designs. These were to executed on tableware, artists initially included Vanessa Bell, John Armstrong, Dod Proctor, Albert Rutherston and Paul Nash. Production of the earthenware examples was entrusted to Colley Shorter, a member of the committee. He immediately delegated the supervision of this to Clarice Cliff, which caused bad feelings between himself and Gordon Forsyth.

Unfortunately, during 1933, it was also to cause animosity between Clarice Cliff and Colley Shorter!

This page:
Moonlight
Bizarre
1933
A stylised blue tree in green and yellow garden, over a lined and chequered setting.
★★★★£££
See also *Devon*.

Opposite:
Nasturtium
Bizarre
1932-1934 (matchings to 1940)
Flowers in red, orange and yellow, by a brown *Cafe-au-Lait* ground.
★★★££

CHAPTER 7

1933
AN INTERRUPTION

The British Industries Fair that was held in February every year, was a key promotional opportunity to secure orders for Clarice Cliff's ware. Many other potbanks in Stoke-on-Trent had to lay-off their decorating departments at this time until they had orders from the Fair, but for Clarice it simply meant an increase in orders. The fair was always visited by the King and Queen as they were keen to promote industry and trade. Every year Queen Mary would buy a few pieces of *Bizarre*; this was generally *Crocus* as she apparently did not like the bolder designs. Ellen Browne was chosen to decorate a special dinner set one year. Never one to miss a promotional angle, Colley Shorter soon added the royal patronage to the factory's notepaper.

A design Queen Mary did not buy in 1933 was *Windbells*. Launched to the trade at the fair, this was soon getting coverage in the national press. "It always looks easy when the expert shows you how", was the caption in an early 1933 newspaper article showing Clarice and some of her girls. Clarice was decorating a *Lotus* jug in her new *Windbells* design, watched by Lily Barrow, Nancy Liversage, Ivy Tunicliff, Lily Dabbs, Marjory Higginson and *Delecia* girl Elsie Nixon. Clarice used her favourite bright orange with green, mustard and blue detail for the tree against a wavy ground.

Windbells was just one of many new designs and shapes Clarice was to issue in 1933, and after the failure of *Le Bon Dieu* in 1932, she returned to the more modern style for her new shapes. A teapot which progressed the geometric style of her *Conical* and *Stamford* shapes was the *Bon Jour*. The round teapot had flat sides, and two cigarette-shaped feet. One of the first designs it was issued in was *Windbells*.

Bon Jour was based on another original shape by Tétard Frères, which in this instance we know Clarice and Colley licenced from them, as we have the memories of a young Eric Grindley who joined the factory in 1932. He witnessed a meeting in the Newport Pottery office between Clarice Cliff, Colley Shorter and a man who was probably Jean Tétard, where the use of the *Bon Jour* shape was negotiated. This had previously been produced in metal, but having made the *Stamford* and *Conical* shapes in earthenware the lessons learnt made it easier to produce elaborate shapes such as this.

The round teapot version was modelled firstly, and appears to have been issued by March 1933, and the shape was registered by the factory - 7782433. Shortly after this an oval coffee-pot was produced, oval water jugs, and a round jampot and biscuit barrel. Each piece was topped with a solid round handle, except for the oval *Bon Jour* sugar dredger, a natural follow-on to the *Conical* sugar dredger which was selling extremely well. The rarest *Bon Jour* shapes are the candlesticks; a single (shape 610) and a double (shape 609) which were made of flat pottery with the round sconces mounted on top, few have survived.

The evolution of *Bon Jour* occurred simultaneously as an important addition was made to Clarice's tableware. The equally exotically named *Biarittz* launched oblong and square plates on the British market. Exactly why Clarice persisted in producing the shape is unclear. They were impractical, more expensive to produce than round plates, which were already selling extremely well. However, her obstinance on this occasion was based in sound commercial instinct. Clarice got such favourable response to the shape that the factory had to persevere, adapting systems to produce it. Again by challenging the known technology she was able to innovate with a shape range that was both technically and aesthetically advanced.

Biarittz dinner sets proved to be as popular for wedding and anniversary presents in 1933 as the *Conical* shape *Early Morning sets* had done in 1929. The demand was so heavy that Clarice had to produce the plates in various sizes and she designed a

Opposite:
Orange Battle
Bizarre
1929-1930
Round orange shapes among vertical green stripes with black splashes flying off.
★★★★★£££££

Top:
Morocco
Bizarre
1928-1929
An early simple abstract, with a curved arch in panels around the ware. Colourways orange and blue.
★★★★★£££

Bottom:
Moselle
Bizarre
1934-1935
Red, green, orange and blue flowers broadly outlined, as a design at the top of ware, similar in style to *Latona* floral designs.
★★★★★££££

Opposite:
Orange House
Fantasque
1930-1932
A cottage with orange walls and black roof with a red, green and yellow tree blown over it.
★★★★££££
See also *Green House*.

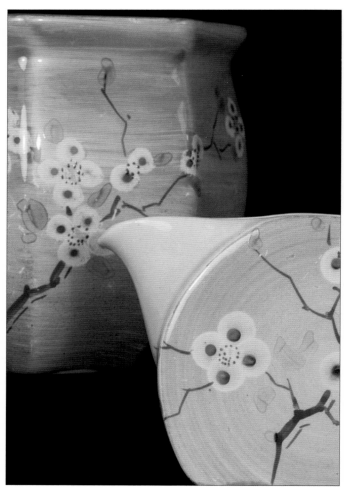

special *Biarittz* tureen. This was inspired by a decorative piece created in trellised metalwork by Josef Hoffmann in 1905. The shape was identical. Clarice simply replaced the four ball bearing feet with tube-like feet from her *Bon Jour* teapot, and added a flat oblong lid that linked the shape to the oblong *Biarittz* plates. The gravy boat was the same shape and doubled as a milk jug, in this guise one appeared in an advertisement for Shredded Wheat cereal.

Young assistant Eric Grindley became heavily involved in the London promotions in 1933. Clarice's main helper was Hilda Lovatt, together they would carefully plan each display or table-setting, Eric witnessed all this and helped out, it was on one of these visits that he first went to the premises of the London agent for *Bizarre* at Andrew's House, Holborn Viaduct.

He described the manager Mr. Frederick Jukes, as "a salesman of the old school, a dapper bespectacled down to earth Londoner. There was not a china and glass wholesaler or retailer across the whole metropolis who was not known by the said Mr. Jukes!" He also recalled that a pair of giant *Yo Yo* vases stood either side of the entrance to the showroom. These were eighteen inches high and decorated in *Latona Red Roses*. Sometimes, as the junior he was told to clean them and remembers they were always full of cigarette ends. The giant *Yo Yo* shape was apparently too big to fit into the normal saggars in the ovens, so only a pair at a time could be fired. Only a few were made as they were just used for shows or publicity purposes, hence their subsequent rarity.

The London showroom, and the numerous exhibitions *Bizarre* appeared at meant that all the larger stores were constantly bombarded with new ware. Throughout the Thirties a team of salesman toured Britain forty-two weeks a year. Apart from Ewart Oakes in the South, there was Godfrey Swift in Scotland and the North, various salesmen covered the Midlands, including Cyril Hind, Ellen Browne's husband. The routine was to travel by train with five casks packed with samples and hold "stock-rooms" at hotels. These were within easy reach of customers who would have already received a postal invitation. The salesman unpacked and displayed the ware on the Monday, took orders until Friday, when he returned to Stoke-on-Trent. He then took the orders to the factory on Saturday morning. This very hard work meant many hours travelling through cold, smoky stations. Ewart Oakes was the only salesman to stay with the company throughout the Thirties.

The increase in demand during 1933 meant the girls in the shops at Newport Pottery were even busier. Their great team spirit and happiness in their work with Clarice is well illustrated by their adaptation of the "Ovaltiney's" song they heard on the radio. The words were still fondly remembered by Mollie Browne sixty years later.

> "*We are the gay Bizookas - happy girls are we*
> *With dabs of paint we're decorating*
> *And for work we're always waiting*
> *Then the stampers will not stamp it*
> *Naughty girls are they*
> *And so we sit and suck our thumbs*
> *Until that great big order comes*
> *So now you know why we're all chums*
> *We're happy girls and boys.*"

The girls left an intriguing puzzle for collectors. Many pieces feature small hand-painted marks, or initials, on the back or base. These were usually made by the paintresses, and the four boy outliners to distinguish their work. Sometimes they were told to do this by Lily Slater, on other occasions they did it when several were painting the same design and they wanted to see how their pieces came out.

It would be nice to think we could use them to name the decorator, but remember that most pieces of ware went though the hands of an outliner, then several enamelers, and then a bander. The colour of the mark may be a clue. Is it in the same colour as the outline, or is it on the enamelling or banding? An 'S' on a piece may be the mark of Sadie Maskrey, and 'H' may be for Harold Walker, and a script 'E' was Eileen Tharme's mark. However, in virtually every case, because decorators changed throughout the Thirties, most initials were used by more than one person. A little

Bottom left:
Lupin
Bizarre
1928
Lupin flowers in *Crocus* colours, this was designed at the same time as *Crocus*, and has the same banding style.
★★★★★£££

Bottom right:
May Blossom
Bizarre
1935-1936
Freehand black spiky tree with blossoms on a yellow and grey streaked ground; produced with yellow, green and pink blossoms.
★★★£

Top:
Newport
Bizarre
1934
Geometric lines and blocks with simple flowers, various colourways including orange and blue.
★★★££

detective work with impressed datemarks and backstamps, and knowledge of the years decorators were at the factory, can give a greater insight into pieces. Remember, however, that many girls have said their mark was a dot, or two dots, or three. Clarice sometimes asked for a salesman's initials to be painted on samples intended for him; you might find "EO" for Ewart Oakes, or "GS" for Godfrey Swift. Part of the charm of these marks is that we can never be certain what they signify.

One design a lot of the girls had worked on was *Idyll*. This had remained in production from 1931, but during 1933 it was moved from the *Appliqué* to the *Fantasque* range, and the original black and red banding was replaced with pastel versions. So many paintresses worked on the design that over the years the lady in crinoline, the tree and the garden were painted in a number of different styles. It is one of the most varied of Clarice's designs.

In March 1933 a strong new design appeared. *Secrets* was to sell as well as *Autumn* had done in 1931. It was a naturally coloured landscape of a hillside with two cottages partly hidden on its brow, a river running past below. A green and yellow tree hung over the whole scene. It was also known by its pattern number 6070, and was produced as an all-over design on many of Clarice's shapes, and as a shoulder pattern on her dinnerware, where even the tureen handles would have a cottage painted on them. The interesting name of *Secrets* may have been chosen sub-consciously by Clarice, as at this time her relationship with Colley Shorter was her secret. It certainly was the subject of much gossip at the factory and in Stoke-on-Trent, and perhaps it was her way of revealing their secret?

Clarice would sometimes drive to Nottingham to stay with Gerty Langford, the china and glass buyer at Griffin & Spaldings store. One location near Clarice's route to Nottingham was Alton Towers, a large ornamental park to the East of Stoke-on-Trent. This may be why in 1933 the *Alton* design appeared. In similar colours to *Secrets* it consisted of foreground trees and flowers, with distant towers. One might postulate that Alton Towers may well have been a suitably private location where

This page:
Nuage
1932
Produced with the same technique as *Cafe-au-Lait* but the paint was thickened to give the surface a texture, design is either full on fancies or a motif on corner of functional ware. Designs include *Bouquet, Oranges* and *Flowers*.
★★★£££

Opposite:
Orange Roof Cottage
Fantasque
1932-1933 (matching to 1938)
A cottage by a bridge with trees and bushes all around.
★★★★££££
See also *Pink Roof Cottage* and page 222.

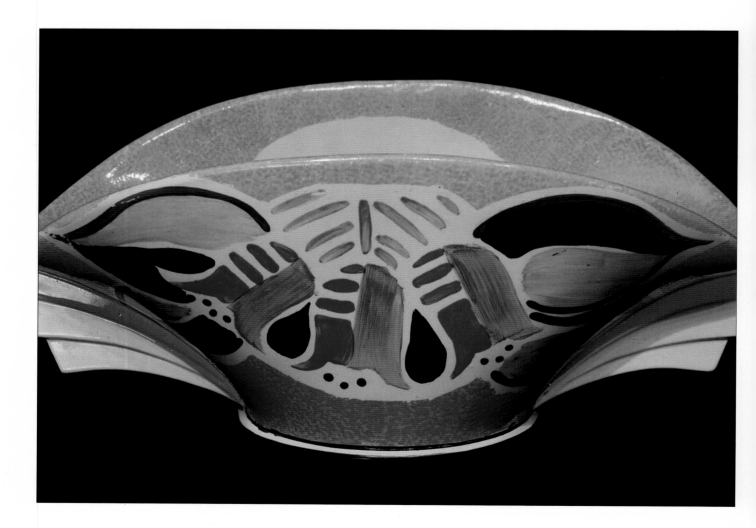

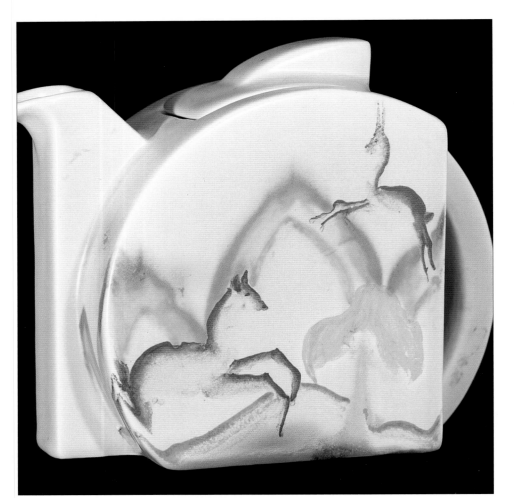

Top:
Opalesque Stencil Deer
Bizarre
1934
A mountain scene with deer, design in blue, brown and yellow.
★★★★★£££

Opposite:
Oranges
Bizarre
1931-1932
Orange fruit with mauve, blue and green leaves.
★★★★£££

Bottom:
Orange/Blue Squares
Bizarre
1929-1930
An extremely bold pattern which is very similar in colour and design to *Cubist* and *Mondrian*. Comprising mainly of straight lines and featuring solid blocks of colour with very heavy black outlines. Although illustrated in the factory shape sheets, very few examples are known.

Cubist, Mondrian and Orange/Blue Squares are all based on designs produced by the artists and architects who supported the Dutch 'De Stijl' movement which was founded in 1917.
★★★★££££

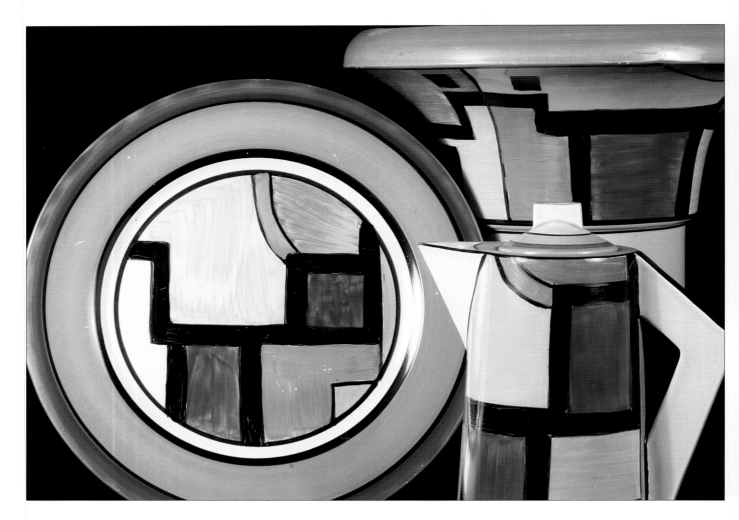

Clarice and Colley went to get away from the business of the factory.

It may just be a coincidence but yet another 1933 landscape also seems to reflect Clarice's life at this time. The design consisted of a bright orange *Bizarre* tree, with a large red bridge crossing from the foreground to the horizon and traversing a swirling grey, green and yellow sea. The design was interestingly named *Solitude*, the implications of this are many. Certainly Clarice was neither able to turn to Colley Shorter or her family, her life hung between them, unresolved, perhaps like the bridge on *Solitude*?

May Avenue was the most interesting of Clarice's new designs in 1933. It featured a row of red-roofed houses half hidden between spade-shaped trees, and a large tree in green and yellow *Cafe-au-Lait* style stippling. Although Clarice chose the name from an avenue just a few streets away from where she was born in Tunstall, the scene was inspired by a painting called *Landscape at Cagnes* by Modigliani. Her awareness and appreciation of art was clearly extremely diverse by this time.

The main significance of *May Avenue* was that it was one of the first designs produced by a new decorating process in the *Bizarre* shop. Previously, the outliners had always used brushes to draw the outline of the design onto ware. Whilst this continued on existing designs, many new designs were outlined with a pen, giving a much finer line. This enabled finer details to be drawn, *May Avenue* is typical of this, in that the landscape has more depth and details, such as the thin lines on the tree. The designs produced with the pen outline process were initially done in black, but later other colours were used. The effect is rather different to the earlier bold, brash landscapes such as *Summerhouse* and *Autumn* but collectors do not differentiate between the two styles, and both are equally collectable.

May Avenue did not sell in large quantities, but the pen outline process was then implemented on the yellow dominated design *Moonlight*, and its stronger colourway *Devon*. However, it was *Coral Firs* a little later in 1933 that proved to be the most popular in the new style. This had fir trees on top of a hill, with a cottage below, white

Opposite:
Oranges & Lemons
Bizarre
1931-1932
Red, orange and yellow fruit with large black leaves in-between.
★★★★£££££

This page:
Orange 'V'
Bizarre
1930-1931
A geometric design in orange, yellow and red, with linear forms between the 'V' shapes.
★★★★£££

cliffs, and in the background a barren landscape. This was perhaps based on the countryside around Stoke-on-Trent, where some of the hills are topped with such trees. The name of the design was taken from the Coral Red colour used on the trunks of the trees.

Coral Firs was an instant good seller, and popular on vases, fancies and tableware right through until 1937. However, although new designs and shapes added further strength to the sales of *Bizarre* and enhanced Clarice's reputation as a designer, the year was to be a difficult one. She had to spend a lot of her time developing the earthenware examples of the *Artists in Industry* pieces which Colley Shorter had agreed to her doing for the Prince of Wales' project. This proved to be a time-consuming task.

The first artists had been chosen by Thomas Acland Fennemore, (then Art Director of E. Brain & Co.,) with Milner Gray and Graham Sutherland. The thirteen included Vanessa Bell, Duncan Grant, Frank Brangwyn and Barbara Hepworth. None of the artists visited Clarice to liaise on how their designs might be transformed to tableware, so she was faced with just water-colour drawings and ink sketches that needed to be adapted onto her standard shapes. Most of the submitted artwork was unsuitable for execution on tableware; vague freehand patterns of flowers, loops, and abstract shapes were strangely ineffective compared to her own hand-painted designs. Clarice had no alternative but to do her best, to produce pieces of the *Artists in Industry* ware she took Ellen Browne off *Bizarre* production, she also used her former bosses Fred Ridgway and John Butler. There is evidence in a letter to Fennemore that Gordon Forsyth resented Clarice's involvement with the project.

"*Such a distinguished bunch of artists should not be used to advertise Clarice Cliff....No one could object to Newport Pottery by Frank Brangwyn R.A., but he (Colley Shorter) should not use Clarice Cliff's name except for pottery designed by her.*"

Forsyth was clearly over-ruled by Colley Shorter, as each piece of the ware had

Opposite:
Palermo
Appliqué
1930-1931
Red-sailed yachts against the sweeping bay of Palermo with a climbing floral plant in the foreground.
★★★★£££££

This page:
With Ethel Timmis as the baby in the pram, the "Bizarre Girls" celebrate the 1936 "Crazy Day".

beneath the artist's facsimile signature: *Produced in Bizarre by Clarice Cliff Wilkinson Ltd.* Colley Shorter credited his designer, her leading brand name and his company.

The pieces were first launched at the *British Industrial Art in Relation to the Home* exhibition at Dorland Hall in Lower Regent Street, London in the summer of 1933. They solicited an unfavourable reaction from both press and public. The project had to continue, however, and luckily Colley had more input at this stage. In an unusual move, he actually co-operated with Gordon Forsyth, together they commissioned further artists. Clarice had to start work on this, a very time-consuming task indeed, as this second series was not unveiled until 1934.

Despite the unfulfilling time she spent on the *Artists in Industry* pieces, Clarice still had a few tricks up her sleeve. A new ware *Goldstone* was invented, featuring a speckled earth coloured body that had a clear glaze. Clarice thought this would encourage a return to more natural shapes. A series of vases, numbered in the early 600 shape sequence were made for *Goldstone*, these were modelled to look as if they had been thrown on a potter's wheel. The shape was called *Lynton*, and matching tea and coffeeware was also produced.

The *Goldstone* glaze was decorated either in simple freehand floral motifs, or patterns of variously coloured thin bands around the ware. The body did not really lend itself to decoration, although *Goldstone* sold well when launched it has not proven collectable yet, as it is rather untypical of her work. However, the *Lynton* tea and coffee ware sold well when issued in designs on a honeyglaze finish.

By late 1933 *Secrets* and *Coral Firs* were selling extremely well, and Clarice added yet more variations to her range. New colourways included *Secrets Orange* and *Blue Firs*. However, again the factory found it hard to achieve her demands. The No. 5 blue used on *Blue Firs* needed a higher firing temperature than the other colours, but the ware was only fired once. This meant that before *Blue Firs* ware left the factory many examples were already losing colour. The workers in the packing shop beneath the *Crocus* shop were even told to wrap it in special paper to stop this happening.

This page:
Parrot Tulip
Sample
1929
Flared tulip flowers and leaves painted freehand. A design known only in the factory sample books at present, but its presence there as a finished watercolour indicates it was definitely produced.

Page 166:
Patina Tree
Bizarre
1932-1933
A tree with bulbous blue or pink foliage.
★★★★£££

Opposite:
Persian (Original)
1928-1929
Isnic designs in hand-painted enamels decorated in the original *Bizarre* style.
★★★★££££

Top:
Patina Tree
See page 164.

Bottom left:
Moderne
Tableware
1929
A partial platinum band with a cartouche featuring a design in print outline, with hand-painted colour, these included: *Norge* (two fir trees), *Odette,* illustrated below (a fruit and flower pattern), *Paysanne* (stylised flowers) and *Jewel* (stylised flowers).
★★★★£

Bottom right:
Mowcop
Clarice Cliff
1937
A small tower amongst trees on a hillock, named after a Staffordshire Victorian folly. A variation on pink glaze known.
★★★★££

Opposite:
Picasso Flower (Red Flower)
Bizarre
1930
A cubist flower with geometric leaves and stems thorough it, colourways orange or red flower with blue centre. Also known with a blue flower and lilac centre.
Colourways:
Orange or Red flower ★★★★££££
Blue flower ★★★★££££
See also page 223.

Honolulu and *Bridgwater*, two new designs again using the pen outline process also appeared. *Honolulu* featured trees with green and black trunks, pendulous red, orange and yellow foliage. Both featured a new style of banding and lining, *Honolulu* having pale green bands, overlaid with strong black lines. Again Clarice hit a commercial note with *Honolulu* and like *Secrets* it was produced on all her shapes as a full pattern, or as a simplified version on tableware.

Bridgwater was an archetypal Clarice Cliff landscape. It took the elements of *Secrets* and adapted them. The cottages overlook a blue and purple river full of colourful reeds, *Secret's* green and yellow tree is replaced with a vivid tree in red and orange. Although *Bridgwater* probably originated in 1933 most examples were produced in the first six months of 1934.

It seems likely that *Honolulu* and *Bridgwater* were just some of many new designs featured at the British Industries Fair early in 1934. In the chronology of Clarice's designs such pieces were often produced late one year for the following year's range. The rate at which change was to affect the Pottery industry was to accelerate in 1934, as Britain came out of the depression and moved into more prosperous times.

Christmas 1933 saw a little more seasonal spirit at the pottery. A Christmas party for the staff was held at the Co-op in Burslem. Clarice and Colley sat at the top table, as the girls joyfully celebrated Christmas together. It was not a free company Christmas party, as they each had to pay two shillings and sixpence - so they made the most of the evening.

Bottom left:
My Garden
1934-1941 and post war
Embossed flowers on decorative and functional ware produced in numerous variations in several series in the 600, 700 and 800 shape ranges. The body of the ware is in various colours which gave the colourways names as follows: *Flame* (red), *Mushroom* (mushroom glaze), *Sunrise* (yellow/brown) and *Verdant* (green).
★★★££ to ★★★££

Bottom right:
Napoli
Clarice Cliff
1937
A garden with a lily pond and tall trees under gold stars, on a mushroom glaze.
★★£

Opposite:
Poplar
Bizarre
1932
One orange and one blue tree with a cottage on the horizon, with large flowers in the foreground.
★★★★££££

Bottom:

Pebbles
Fantasque
1929-1930
A cluster of multi-coloured circles in panels with zig zag shapes in an orange or blue ground.
★★★★££££

Top:

Pink Roof Cottage
Fantasque
1932-1933
A pink roofed cottage with yellow and green walls, by a bridge with light green and blue trees and bushes all around.
★★★★★£££££
See also *Orange Roof Cottage*.

Opposite:

Propeller
Bizarre
1931
Extremely stylised flowers looking like a ship's propeller, with a contour line effect between.
★★★★★££££

CHAPTER 8

1934
A CREATIVE DILUTION

With the *Bon Jour* and *Biarritz* ranges selling extremely well, and the *Secrets*, *Honolulu* and *Coral Firs* designs becoming best sellers during 1934, Clarice Cliff and Colley Shorter were free to devote much of the year to the *Artists in Industry* project. However, it seems that whereas Colley thought Clarice's involvement would be prestigious for his designer, Clarice regarded it negatively. Although he felt justified to want to associate her name with such well-known artists, Clarice created spontaneously and saw her work on the project as a predetermined commitment.

However, simpler problems also had to be solved, one of which was that Clarice had to find new staff as her original girls left. During the year outliner Annie Beresford and enameller Florrie Winkle married and left to have families. Although Lily Slater supervised the girls Clarice still took a personal interest in selecting new paintresses. She believed in taking girls straight from school: Edna Cheetham, Vera Parr, Katie Hulme and Doris Johnson were among the new recruits. Doris's memories of her first meeting with Clarice are interesting:

"*I had taken in my two hand-painted plates with me which I had done at Art School, and Clarice was instantly very pleased with them. She said, 'Oh yes, very nice, you can start work on Monday'. The interview was over very quickly, but I was glad, it was just what I wanted. Clarice was lovely; I liked her immediately, she had no airs and graces, you could talk with her straight away.*"

Doris Johnson's memories of a soft Clarice contrast with the more severe person

This page:
Pink Tree
Fantasque
1934
A cloud-shaped tree with pink foliage, in a wood with yellow roofed cottages.
★★★★★£££

Opposite:
Red Roofs
Bizarre
1931-1932
A cottage with an orange flowered climber up its side, in front of a tall green tree, with a fence running by, and a giant orange flower on the reverse.
★★★★£££££

some of the other girls remember, but of course Clarice was now thirty-five years old, and seemed to have mellowed towards the younger girls.

Impetus was added to the sales of *Honolulu*, when Clarice issued it in a blue and pink colourway, which she called *Rudyard*. Having named the original after an exotic location thousands of miles away, *Rudyard* was named after a Stoke-on-Trent beauty spot. As it used the No. 5 blue many examples suffer from the same problems as *Blue Firs*. Some delicate patterns appeared at this time using the pen outline process. The *Hydrangea* design appeared in orange and green colourways, and *Japan* featured an exotic tree by a pagoda and pool and was produced in blue and green colourways. These designs were less stylish than others issued in 1934 and did not sell well.

Clarice was to spend a vast amount of 1934 working on the *Artists in Industry* project, which was not to be exhibited until late in December. This inevitably reduced the time she had to be creative, and may have been one reason why she moved towards more natural browns and greens in her work. The list of artists had been enlarged and Clarice had to work with over twenty, some of whom had two or three different designs to be adapted to tableware. New artists included Laura Knight, her sister Eva Crofts, Allan Walton and even Gordon Forsyth. A major problem Clarice had with this project was that she had little feedback from the artists themselves who with one exception seemed content to submit their water-colour drawings and collect their fee. The exception was Laura Knight.

Clarice Cliff and Laura Knight had met on a train at some stage prior to the project, and it seems they got on well. Born in Long Eaton in Nottingham, Laura Knight had lived in Yorkshire, Cornwall and London by this time, and during 1928 she had lived with Carmo's circus. This was to get inspiration for her work, which included a number of sketches and oils painted in situ. These impressions of the circus were to provide the inspiration for her *Circus* tableware. Each plate had a different performer in the centre, surrounded by a sea of faces making the circus ring. The amount of work the factory and Laura Knight put into modelling these is evident in Eric Grindley's recollections.

Bottom left:
Nemesia
Bizarre
1930
A printed outline of small flowers in the corners or handles of ware, enamelled in yellow, orange and green.
★★££

Bottom right:
New Flag
Bizarre
1929
An early variation of *Original Bizarre* given a separate name.
★★★£££

Opposite:
Red Tree
Appliqué
1930-1931
On a green, black and orange striped ground, a tree with black and red saucer shaped fruit, against a grey sky.
★★★★★£££££

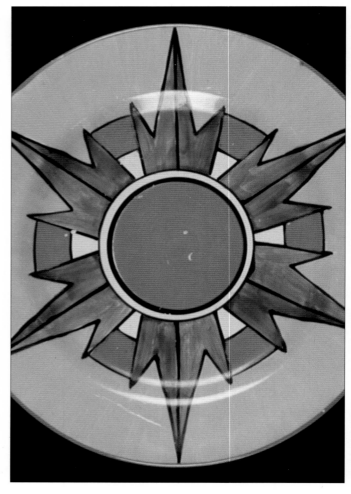

Bottom left:
Anemone
Clarice Cliff
1937-1938
Freehand flowers painted realistically, a
rim decoration on vases or a full motif
on vases, sometimes with runnings.
★★★£

Bottom right:
Passion Fruit
Clarice Cliff
1936
A twig heavy with pink and lilac, or yellow
and blue fruit and flowers, seen on a
turquoise glaze as well as honeyglaze.
★★£

Top:
Ravel
Tableware
1929-1936
Simple cubist flowers and leaves in jade
and orange as a motif on dinner, tea and
coffee ware.
Colourways:
Green ★££
Blue ★★★£££
See also *Brunella*.

Opposite:
Rodanthe
See page 178.

"*Laura Knight had been to the factory on a flying visit, for a meeting as to how her ware was to be produced. A few months later when we were down in London for a trade show I was asked by Clarice to take some of the models across to her. I took the clay models for the vegetable dish and the gravy boat shapes for her to approve. I went on the tube, carefully carrying them to Laura Knight's house at Langford Place, in St. John's Wood. I was taken into the morning room by the servant, then she came in to inspect them, and after a few minutes we had tea and biscuits. The models had been made from her designs by our main modeller Joe Woolliscroft. She made several adjustments, and marked them with indelible pencil where she wanted them altering, and wrote notes to Clarice.*"

Circus ware was costly to produce, and extremely expensive when sold and has remained so ever since. Apart from the Laura Knight range the others were not to attract favourable publicity when launched later in 1934.

One outcome from Clarice's involvement with *Artists in Industry* was that she experimented with ceramic crayons. These were used on biscuit ware with the glaze then applied over the design. Clarice chose outliner Rene Dale to do very English landscape scenes in natural colours. The range was called *Crayon Scenes* and at least a dozen designs were issued, and they were sold as decorative items primarily on plates.

Erin was an unusual design that appeared in 1934. It was an abstract scene, with a cloud shaped tree in the foreground, and water lily shapes floating above. These resembled the water lilies from the *Chintz* design. The banding on *Erin* was done as shading, and this again marked a change in Clarice's work. *Erin* was the mythological name for Ireland and the choice of green and orange as the colourways may hold more significance than is obvious at first.

Biarritz dinnerware continued to sell well in 1934. One design was simply the customer's initials hand-painted in a platinum finish onto rims, and these proved popular as wedding and anniversary presents. *Biarritz* plates were also painted in

This page:
Red Tulip (Tulip & Leaves)
Fantasque
1930-1931
A single, bold tulip in red with green leaves and yellow, blue and black detail.
★★★★£££

Page 177:
Rhodanthe
Bizarre and Clarice Cliff
1934-1941
A freehand design with large marigold flowers in orange and brown, on sinuous brown stems painted in the etching style.
★££
See also *Aurea* and *Viscaria*.

Opposite:
Rudyard
Bizarre
1933-1934
A tree with light and dark green trunk, with pink and blue pendulous foliage. Named after the beauty spot north of Stoke-on-Trent.
★★★££££
See also *Honolulu*.

standard *Bizarre* designs, as decorative wall plates to go with a *Bon Jour* teaset in the same pattern. Changes in trade restrictions, plus a natural demand for the *Biarritz* shape in North America finally gave Colley Shorter a break into that market. It sold continuously until 1939.

In July Clarice developed a new range that was to be as successful in 1934 as *Crocus* had been in 1928. She introduced *My Garden* which was a world away from her geometric shapes, but it was a logical one as she loved flowers, and was forever poring over her gardening books in her studio. The *My Garden* idea was simple, vases and jugs rising out of a sea of flowers, with floral handles. The flowers were highly modelled, hand-painted in enamels, the body of the ware was given just a hint of colour. We know that Clarice Cliff supervised the modelling of these pieces, but the work was mainly done by Harold Walker and John Shaw. They did the original pieces so well that even when the moulds were made from these, and pieces cast, the quality of modelling was better than most comparable ware being made in this style in the Potteries at the time. One of the reasons *My Garden* was such a good line for the factory was that it was easy for apprentices to decorate as the colours of the flowers were contained by the moulding.

Clarice introduced *My Garden* in July at the *Daily Mail Ideal Home Exhibition*. It was well received, and gained her yet more coverage in the national press, where she was mentioned as, "Clarice Cliff the only woman art director in the pottery trade".

As *My Garden* flourished, so *Fantasque* withered. The brash and very British landscapes that had dominated the range had sold well since 1930, but in what was to be the direction for the rest of the Thirties, it disappeared in a rationalisation. As early as December 1933 new landscapes had appeared with a *Bizarre* mark that would previously have been given a *Fantasque* one on stylistic grounds. The *Fantasque* designs continued to be available, but were now issued just marked *Bizarre by Clarice Cliff*. It was some time before ware with the *Fantasque* mark was to disappear from stockists, as late as 1936 the name was still being used in the factory order books.

This page:
Scraphito
1930-1932
A range of vases with deeply moulded abstract design over all of the body, broadly painted in a number of different colours, sometime using a silver colour.
★★★★££

Opposite:
Secrets
Bizarre
1933-1937
A river estuary next to a green hill topped by two brown roofed cottages, and a tree with green and yellow foliage in the foreground, also pattern number 6070. *Secrets Orange* is a bold colourway with a yellow and blue tree with purple added to the foreground and orange banding.
Full design ★★£££
Shoulder pattern ★★££
Orange ★★★★£££

Perhaps Clarice's most inspired work of 1934 was of some changes to her *Conical* ware. She updated the seemingly perfect *Yo Yo* vase and *Conical* bowl, inspired by the work of Margarete Heymann-Loëbenstein. Known as Greta, she was a German ceramic designer trained at the Bauhaus. During the Twenties her work was stocked by *Heal's* in London, and from these shapes Clarice "borrowed" a simple device of a handle made of two solid round shapes of slightly different sizes. Clarice used this to replace the oblong side supports of the *Yo Yo* vase and the triangular feet on *Conical* bowls. These pieces were stunning, but perhaps a little out of synch with the tastes of the 1934 customer and judging by their subsequent rarity did not sell well.

Another new style of hand-painting was originated by Clarice Cliff in 1934. After the brash brushstrokes of original *Bizarre*, then the pen outline introduced in 1933 she moved to more naturally decorated designs when she introduced ware with etched brushstrokes. Complementary colours were skilfully shaded into each other, and this was decorated freehand with no outline. The most successful design using this technique was undoubtedly *Rhodanthe*. This featured tall orange and yellow marigold style flowers, on sinuous brown stems. The design was popular immediately, but was a world away from the geometric shapes Clarice was still producing. This means that ironically it was even produced on *Yo Yo* vases, *Biarritz* ware and *Conical* teapots. This incongruous combination was yet another fact that made her ware *Bizarre*.

One range that was not successful in 1934 was *Opalesque*. This was the name of a glaze and decoration technique in the *Inspiration* style. The decoration was done with liquid metallic oxides, but it lacked the depth of colour and surface of *Inspiration* and the designs were simpler. Most examples were decorated in versions of existing designs, the main exception was *Stencil Deer*.

The 1934 show at the *Holborn Restaurant* again used showbiz personalities to promote the ware those attending were Lesley Henson, Bobby Howes, Gertrude Lawrence and members of the Crazy Gang. The press were invited to attend and in the following week articles and photographs appeared in all the daily newspapers and

Opposite:
Sliced Circle
Bizarre
1929-1930
A geometric design of radiating lines and circles, the circles are displaced either side of a line. Produced in orange, yellow, green and blue, with irregularly coloured segments.
Colourways:
Green/Yellow ★★★★££££
Red/Blue ★★★★★£££££

This page:
Sliced Fruit
Bizarre
1930
A band of stylised sliced fruit showing their segments, in orange, yellow and brown, or blue, mauve and green.
★★★£££

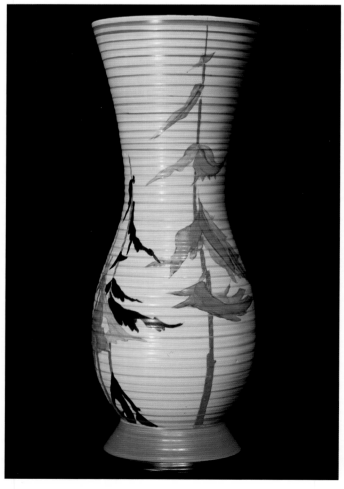

women's magazines. Eric Grindley recalled that the result of all this publicity was a big increase in home and export sales. He said, "Despite the fourteen hour working days, I found it was a real treat and of invaluable experience to go to prestige shows and have contact with so many personalities and trades people!"

Clarice remained her unpredictable self when she made some new shapes late in 1934 that were very Art Deco. A series of vases were based on the shape of her *Bon Jour* teapot. The smallest was just a flat-sided, round vase, with cigarette shaped feet supporting it. The *Double Bon Jour* vase consisted of medium and large versions of the same shape, one in front of the other. Then, by joining the *Single* on to the *Double*, she had a *Triple Bon Jour* vase which had two wells for water. The vases were numbered 674-1, 2 and 3 respectively. The shape was stylish, but stretched the capabilities of the clay body to the extreme. Many examples have fine hairline cracks, particularly the *Triple* where the two halves are joined together. Because of this the shape is rare, and the few examples known are in later designs.

The *Triple Bon Jour* vase completed the circle, in that the basic concept of its shape was the 366 vase of 1929 put on its side. In returning to the pure geometric forms Clarice Cliff was really finishing the natural design progression of the 1929 pieces that had got lost in the rush.

During 1934 Clarice produced a new addition to her teaware range. Having used the circle, tube and square, the natural option was for a triangular theme. The shape was called *Trieste* and the flat sided teapot was triangular in profile with rounded edges. A special milk and sugar were made for the set, with three sided plates and saucers, but with the *Conical* shape cups. The shape is an extremely strong one, with its softened Art Deco styling. However, by this time, the more Art Deco designs had been discontinued, so it is mainly found in muted colours, although some examples in *Coral Firs* are known. It appeared after the more naturally shaped *Lynton* and so is a strange hark back to the *Bizarre* era, that by this time was drawing to a close.

December 1934 saw the launch of the *Artists in Industry* ware in an exhibition at Harrods store in London, called *Modern Ware for the Table*. Despite being opened by Sir William Rotherstein, President of the Royal Academy of Arts, and gaining a lot of publicity the verdict of the public was negative. The influential *Studio* publication said, "It must be regretfully noted that some of the designs were quite unsuited to the purpose for which they were intended." Ironically, Laura Knight's work paid off, as Eric Grindley recalled, "It was only really *Circus* that sold." Such ware was not really a viable proposition, however, and it was only the likes of film-star Gracie Fields who could afford the £70 cost of a twelve person *Circus* dinnerset.

Bottom left:
Pine Grove
Bizarre and Clarice Cliff
1935
Boldly drawn black and blue fir trees, covered with thin blue lines, also pattern number 6499.
★★★££

Bottom right:
Pink Pearls
Clarice Cliff
1936-1937
A thin tree trunk with pink and blue fruit, pink and red flowers around the base.
★★★★★£

Top:
Solomon's Seal
Bizarre
1930
A simple printed floral outline of a sprig of stylised Solomon's Seal flowers, coloured in lilac, blue and green.
This is often confused with Canterbury Bells.
★★££

CHAPTER 9

1935
THE MAGIC FADES?

In January 1935 Clarice Cliff was 36 years old. In the Thirties this was regarded as almost middle-aged, but Clarice did not act that way. The majority of her time was spent dashing from her flat at Snow Hill to the works in her Austin car. Even if she had not been one of the few women to have a car and drive herself she would still have attracted a lot of attention from local people. Her stylish dress sense, her Liberty silk scarves, her single lifestyle, all made people she came in to contact with aware that she was different.

With Clarice's work on the production of the *Artists in Industry* ware finished, it was now the job of the sales department to sell the earthenware side of the project. Colley Shorter recruited his nephew Bill Crawford to the company, to organise shows in the china departments of various customers. The show spent a week at Barrow's in Birmingham from February 12th, then moved to Midland Drapery in Derby on the 22nd and was in Sheffield from March 18th at the John Walsh store. Despite lack of sales, the factory persisted in promoting the ware as it had invested so much time and money in it.

The financial restrictions of the depression had been left behind by 1935, and Clarice was enjoying the fruits of her labours. In July she treated herself to a new car. She went for the top of the range Austin Seven Pearl Cabriolet. The basic car was £100, but her cabriolet version, complete with custom grey paintwork cost £197. Only a few of the managers at Newport Pottery had cars, even the work's director only had

Opposite:
Solitude
Fantasque
1933
An orange and black tree in the foreground, with a red bridge rising behind which crosses a green, yellow and grey sea.
★★★★££££

This page:
Stile & Trees
Clarice Cliff
1937
A country stile with trees and bushes either side, painted in naturalistic colours.
★★★★££

186 R.

Top:
Sungold
Bizarre
1934
Yellow and amber triangular wedges, in
pastel shades, similar to the *Original Bizarre*
but much lighter.
★★★££
See also *Killarney.*

Bottom:
Sunray Leaves
Bizarre
1929
Alternating panels of jade sunrays with
orange sunrays, with stylised stems and
leaves painted on them.
★★★★£££

Opposite:
Trees & House (Alpine)
See page 190.

a torpedo shaped three wheeler, so Clarice's new car took people's breath away, and caused more gossip!

By 1935, the *Bizarre* girls were able to enjoy a good social life away from the factory. The Grand Hotel in Hanley was a favourite haunt on Monday nights when they had dancing lessons. All the girls loved the cinema, and in the summer paintresses Mollie Browne and Edna Cheetham regularly played tennis with their boyfriends. Now they were older, the girls were sent away for longer periods for demonstrations. Rene Dale went to Plummer Roddis at Hastings, and stores at Brixton, Great Yarmouth, Welwyn Garden City and Liverpool. During the Welwyn Garden City demonstration a man approached her and showed interest in the hand-painting technique. After she had chatted to him for a while, he asked if she knew who he was. When she said she had no idea, he said, "I'm Henry Moore, the sculpture outside the centre is mine."

After the *Artists in Industry* project Clarice's style changed, as did the demand for bright ceramics. *Coral Firs* and *Secrets* remained popular, but customers in the second half of the Thirties showed a preference for a softer palette of colours, more formal designs, and ware with floral motifs. Sales of geometric shapes declined, modelled ranges such as *My Garden* were more in demand, so Clarice continued to adapt and enlarge them.

As demand for *Rhodanthe* grew, new colourways were introduced: *Viscaria* was produced in dominant pink, a blue colourway was called *Aurea*. The etching technique was also to be utilised for other designs: *Sandon* and *Fragrance* were two different colourways of the same tree and garden scene, from these came *Trallee* which added a cottage with open shutters, the blue sky pouring out of its chimney. All these designs lack the strong rim or edge banding that had acted as a frame for Clarice's abstracts and landscapes, helping collectors differentiate between the early designs and later ones.

However, 1935 was not just the year that Clarice lost the colour from her palette, it

Pages 189, 190, 191, 195.

Trees & House (Alpine)
Fantasque
1929-1931
A landscape with a bubble tree, a wedge tree and a half hidden cottage.
The rarest variation is the colourway with blue grass from 1931.
Colourways:
Orange ★★★£££
Red ★★★★££££
7 colour (pastel) ★★★£££

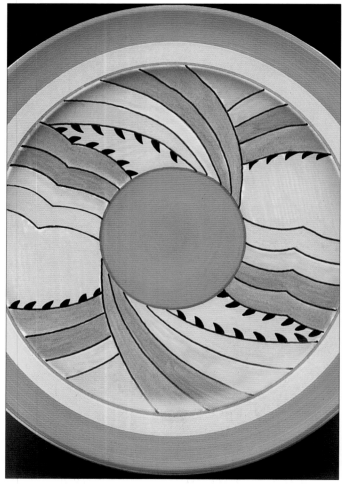

was more importantly the year a whole range of her shapes ceased production. The Art Deco inspired shapes she had designed between 1929 and 1933, were gradually phased out as the factory rationalised its range. It may be that the moulds for these shapes were getting worn, so it was not worth investing in more, but it seems more likely that the market had changed, as a new generation of young adults shopped for tableware and fancies.

Staff changes in the *Bizarre* shop may have been instrumental in the move away from the *Bizarre* style. The two key boy outliners Harold Walker and John Shaw left at this time, as they had both been promised they would be designers when they joined. Although they were allowed to do this from time to time, they never received credit for their work. The matchings of early Thirties designs produced after they left are noticeably different to the originals.

The sales of *Bizarre* in the London area were also affected by the loss of Frederick Jukes from the showroom. He retired and was succeeded by a Mr. Sergeant. Eric Grindley remembered him as "a fast talking southern type of salesman", who found Mr Jukes, "a hard act to follow." Consequently London sales suffered. Ewart Oakes remained as Southern area salesman, but changes also took place in the North at this time, with Ellen Browne's husband Cyril Hind taking over the area.

The demands of overseas buyers may also have affected the new designs and shapes Clarice was to issue. Colley Shorter's work on exports had paid dividends, as he had enlarged the number of overseas agents and by 1935 ware was sent to Brazil, Cuba, Norway, Holland and Belgium, for a while they even had a Swiss agent. These agents were also offered the output of Shorter & Sons, which sold well in existing markets such as Australia and New Zealand.

Colley Shorter spent many weeks abroad establishing overseas agents and organising shows. During these times his wife Annie generally remained at Chetwynd House and was rarely seen. She only left the house, to go on tours of the Staffordshire countryside driven by the chauffeur Herbert Webb. Annie's eldest daughter Margaret was twenty-three by 1935 and was well aware of her father's closeness to Clarice. She recalled that her mother knew about it but, "would not have it mentioned in the house." By 1935 Annie Shorter was an invalid and was admitted to hospital at Market Drayton.

The economy in Britain by this time was much healthier than it had been when *Bizarre* and *Fantasque* were at their peak. With this new found financial confidence, came a change in public taste, perhaps stimulated by the war that most people accepted was inevitable. Were the Jazz Age colours and shapes too racy for the new buyers? Certainly, we know from surviving examples that many shapes were discontinued. Production of *Conical* and *Stamford* teapots gradually ceased, as did many of the 1928 to 1932 vase shapes. The popular *Bon Jour* tea and coffee ware continued as it matched the *Biarritz* tableware, but was issued mainly in lightly decorated designs.

The *Bizarre by Clarice Cliff* logo was still being used in the companies' advertisements in *Pottery Gazette and Glass Trade Review* in September. This announced their "Annual Pottery Display in the Holborn Restaurant from September 2nd to 16th". However, the *Bizarre* name seemed out of place alongside a photograph of traditionally shaped *Delph* dinner ware in design 6339, a shoulder pattern of curved lines and a minute floral motif.

By 1935, the factory was so well organised that we have more complete records about the designs issued. Many had both names and pattern numbers, it seems likely that these were issued sequentially by this time, so they give an insight into the development of designs. The *Blue Crocus* colourway, design number 6393, appeared in September 1935, and surprisingly was mainly sold just in the south-east of England. Then, came pattern 6614, a design with nearly all the shocking elements of Clarice's early success. It had all-over colour, a cottage and trees, and a sky in *Delecia* style. It seems the original colourway may have been the *Newlyn* one which had the more orthodox blue sky, but almost immediately another colourway was produced with a rich-red sky, that was called *Forest Glen*. In retrospect it almost appears as a symbolic red curtain coming down on all that made *Bizarre* and Clarice Cliff unique.

Bottom left:
Shark's Teeth
Bizarre
1930
Curved shapes in orange, brown and mustard, with teeth shapes along the edge.
Based on an original pochoir by French designer Edouard Benedictus.
★★★★££££

Bottom right:
Silver Birch
Clarice Cliff
1937
A tree with green foliage and mottled white trunk, and a chocolate and amber coloured hill.
★★★★★££

Top:
Sunshine
Bizarre
1931
A printed brown outline of flowers enamelled in yellow and brown.
★★★££

Top and bottom:
Sunrise
Fantasque
1929-1930
A stylised sunray motif next to wavy lines, and clusters of circles, colourways orange, red and blue.
★★★★£££££

Opposite:
Trees & House (Alpine)
See page 190.

CHAPTER 10

1936-1972
AFTER BIZARRE

Forest Glen neatly straddles the period when the *Bizarre* trade name disappeared. For the first half of 1936 *Forest Glen* with a *Bizarre* mark was sold extensively throughout Britain, and continued in production with just a *Clarice Cliff* mark into 1937. Strangely, the design appears to be have been very popular at a time when the factory was moving away from strident colours.

Clarice's move to natural colours and forms from 1936 was perhaps a reflection of the sombre mood in Britain. Apart from the threat of war, the death of King George V in January, set the tone for the year. The uncertainty of the situation between the un-crowned Edward VIII and his American confidante Mrs. Simpson was foremost in people's minds. Perhaps Clarice and Colley realised that the *Bizarre* days were over as their customers did not want surprising any more.

Clarice's designs took on a simpler palette, the landscapes were only lightly decorated and lacked the banding that had given Clarice's work its distinguishing frame. *Taormina* had a tree by a cliff edge; *Lorna* was a countryside scene, complete with bridge and cottage, but was executed in reserved colours. *Brookfields* was a cottage next to ploughed fields and a bridge, the whole design was covered with fine concentric lines in blue and yellow. *Chalet* was a detailed garden scene with individual dots of colour for the flowers either side of the path leading to the chalet.

Few of the landscapes sold strongly, which did not matter as *Rhodanthe* and its variations were still very popular. *Honeydew* and *Sundew* were produced on the

This page:
Tartan
Bizarre
1934
A simple tartan pattern produced by very fine lining, in several colourways, primarily seen on *Trieste* shape table and teaware.
★★★★££

Rhodanthe theme to give a dealer in the south-west of England exclusive designs, decorated en-masse by teams of girls. Doris Johnson recalled it was still the noisiest and liveliest part of the factory.

"*At lunchtimes we used to sit where we worked, and as she was so small we used to dress up Ethel Timmis in all sorts of fancy outfits, a wedding dress, a cowboy outfit etc., we did have a lot of fun!*"

Ethel was also the focal point of the Crazy Day parade in 1936, which was to raise money for the Hayward Hospital in Burslem. The float was more basic than the earlier ones. The girls dressed as maternity nurses, held dolls, and in a pram in the centre sat Ethel Timmis as a baby. An unimaginative sign on the back just named Wilkinson's and Newport; the flair of the early Thirties floats had gone.

During 1936 the missus Lily Slater, a key member of staff, left. Clarice replaced her with paintress Alice Andrews, whose firm but friendly style, aided by her height, kept the girls in hand. Alice was pleased with her new job, as she "preferred running about rather than sitting", and remembers that she "got five shillings extra."

One can date the introduction of the *Clarice Cliff* mark to the *Pottery Gazette and Glass Trade Review* of the 1st August 1936. An advertisement in a similar format to the one in September 1935 again confusingly mixed some of Clarice's ware with that of Shorter & Sons., but this time the logo next to some unimaginative *Lynton* tableware just read: *Clarice Cliff.*

The royal abdication in December brought a sad end to the year in which *Bizarre* also abdicated. The week of the crisis, the girls endlessly debated whether the King should be allowed to marry Mrs. Wallis Simpson. They were so vocal that at the end of the week Clarice gave them a ticking off and docked wages from a few girls! Was her sensitivity about this related to her own emotional position being unresolved?

Clarice relinquished some of the modelling she had enjoyed so much when she took

Bottom left:
Some examples of the stylish advertising printed in women's magazines of the early Thirties for *Clarice Cliff* and *Bizarre* ware.

Bottom right:
Sir Malcolm Campbell appearing at a *Bizarre* promotion, pictured with Colley Shorter and the *Bizooka* in September 1931 in London.

on apprentice modellers Betty Silvester and Peggy Davies. Clarice and Colley chose Peggy after seeing her end of term work at Burslem School of Art. These modellers were to make a significant contribution to Clarice's output. Peggy modelled a series of face masks, the *Heads of Nations* that were issued with a *Clarice Cliff* mark in 1937; Betty also designed a mass of teapot and bookend shapes. Her intelligently modelled *Showgirl* and *Student* bookends were only produced in small quantities, but her innovative *Teepee* teapot was to be produced after the war and sold very well in Canada.

Clarice simplified the designs on her tableware; a mass of motifs, shoulder patterns and simple banded designs were originated. *Biarritz* tableware was produced with just a sophisticated gold line around its geometric shapes. Many of the designs were just given pattern numbers, but some were bestowed more sophisticated names such as *Kensington*, *Piccadilly* and *Vienna*.

Ironically, many of the early Thirties designs were still popular, the 1937 factory ledgers have orders for *Autumn* and *Orange Roof Cottage*. One order from A. J. Pepper of Birmingham even requested some *Age of Jazz* figures. These were apparently to be used as a wall decoration in a restaurant, so the order instructed, "Pierce a hole each side of the figure as the sample sent." Not long after this even these symbols of the Jazz Age were to be lost. Eric Grindley remembers that the factories remaining stock of plain figures was just one of many old shapes to be consigned to the shard-ruck on the other side of the Trent-Mersey canal.

Clarice Cliff was moving towards her fortieth birthday at a time when the country was preparing itself for war. Almost in anticipation of the need for security, Clarice moved into what we might call her cosy period. She produced gently moulded shapes based on natural forms, such as *Corncob* and *Raffia*. These were complementary to the still successful *My Garden*. Every year until the war variations were added by changing the colour of the body, ranges included *My Garden Verdant* and *My Garden Flame*. The factory also introduced a number of softly coloured glazes; a mushroom

Opposite:
Swirls
Fantasque
1930
Black overlapping curved lines forming a pattern in which segments are differently coloured in orange, blue, yellow, red and lilac.
★★★★£££££

Left:
Tartan Poppy (Hatched Rose)
Bizarre
1935
A stylised poppy with the petals completely covered in tartan style hatching, and the piece then covered in fine bands around the edge.
★★★££

Right:
Tree
Fantasque
1929
A very simple stylised tree with orange trunk and green and blue pendulous foliage.
One of the first Fantasque designs, this has the design name hand-painted on some pieces.
★★★★★£££

glaze was used extensively on many shapes from chargers to wall masks, an apple green glaze was also popular.

A whole range called *Water Lily* appeared in 1938 and was produced both before and after the war. The shape 973 *Water Lily* bulb bowl was a massive seller, being produced in large quantities for the home market and abroad. Even more traditional was the *Celtic Harvest* range with its embossed sheaves of corn, and handles modelled as bunches of fruit. Sales of the last few landscapes persisted as the modelled ware became dominant, these included *Clovelly* (6932), and *Stile & Trees* (6933).

The designs and shapes after *Bizarre*, only needed enamelling so the need for outliners and bander and liners diminished. This happened at a time when many of the girls were leaving anyway. The original *Crocus* girl Ethel Barrow, and Mary Brown left to have families followed shortly after by Cissy Rhodes, Phyllis Tharme and *Delecia* girl Elsie Nixon. Clarice was always sad when her favourites left as she had clearly grown attached to them and whilst she had always been a tough boss, she had earned their respect.

By 1939 there were just forty girls in the *Bizarre* shop and with war imminent the trade show was held at the London showrooms at Holborn Viaduct. Then on Sunday, September 3rd 1939, came the announcement of war. Newport Pottery and Wilkinson's were initially busy as production switched to hotel ware, tableware and ware for the troops. Key staff left to help the war effort including Eric Grindley and Stan Critchlow who enlisted in the army. Their replacement was a young boy who was to play a major role at the factory for 23 years. He was soon involved in working with both the packers and in the office at Newport, in the process he became very close to Clarice and Colley. His name was Norman Smith.

It was a few months before Clarice's paintresses began to leave, to work either in munitions' factories or in the Forces. Soon, the only *Bizarre* girls left were Clara Thomas, Mary Moses, Mollie Brown, Beth Evans, Eileen Tharme, Edna Cheetham, Winnie Pound, Marjory Higginson, Cissy Rhodes and Ethel Timmis. Hand-painted

Opposite:
Tennis
Bizarre
1930-1931
Apart from the design which does not resemble any other produced by the factory the most striking aspect of this pattern is the use of an unusual combination of colours and the minimal use of black. Without the usual black outline, straight and curved broad lines in green, blue, red, yellow, grey and lilac all interlock on a honeyglaze background. On some larger pieces such as a *Lotus* jug, a yellow cloud effect is added to the top to reduce some of the background. Hollow ware such as vases, jugs, tea or coffee pots sometimes have little or no banding, whilst plates or saucers are usually found profusely banded.
The similarity of the 'net' motif used in both Tennis and Football sometimes results in the incorrect name being attributed.
★★★★£££££

This page:
Tulips
Clarice Cliff
1934-1935
The original name of this design is misleading as the tulips are just a small part of this garden scene with a tree, a cottage and tulips in the distance.
It is essentially the Idyll design without the crinoline lady.
★★★£££

ware continued to be produced as evidenced by examples of *Rhodanthe* and *Nasturtium* with impressed datemarks of 1940. As well as hand-painting and lithography the girls helped in other departments, backing the war effort by knitting for the troops and practising first-aid during their lunch break.

The most significant event for Clarice Cliff and Colley Shorter, in the first few months of the war, was that in November 1939 Colley's wife Annie died in hospital at Market Drayton after her long illness. There was a quiet funeral and immediately afterwards Clarice and Colley became inseparable. One Saturday, whilst drinking at the Pub in Burslem with some friends from the pottery industry, Colley Shorter was told by Edward Wenger, a close friend, "It's about time you married that girl." In 1940 it was not acceptable to marry so quickly after the death of your wife, but Colley Shorter ignored this and in his usual headstrong way asked Clarice to marry him. They wed on 21st December 1940 but only a few family members were told. The marriage was kept secret for the best part of a year. Even Ewart Oakes who had long been a friend of Clarice's, did not know about it until she wrote him a letter a year later on 10th December 1941.

> "*I have been trying to sneak ten minutes to write to you for the last several days, and this is my first chance.... I have a bit of news for you which may not come as much of a surprise - Colley and I are married - this at the moment is not generally known, but I know that you can be discreet.*"

The few remaining *Bizarre* girls were then told of the marriage, Marjory Higginson recalls that she asked, "Do we call you Mrs. Shorter now?" Clarice replied, "No, no. Miss Cliff will do nicely." The girls were very pleased for her, but although some of Clarice's family were to get to know Mr. Colley, they never really met his family.

Initially, Clarice and Colley tried to perpetuate their pre-war routine. Norman Smith remembers that he would take letters to Newport Pottery for signature by Colley Shorter every afternoon. Clarice and Colley always had tea together at 3.30 in her

Opposite:
Sunspots
Bizarre
1930-1931
A combination of Art Deco, Egyptian and Aztec motifs consisting of wavy lines, triangles, circles and dots all interlocking to produce a vibrant design. Whilst contemporary with *Carpet* which is found with orange or red as the main colour, *Sunspots* is known only from examples using red.
Although photographs of this pattern exist in the archives, examples of this design have only recently been found and are extremely rare.
★★★★★££££

This page:
Taormina
Bizarre
1936-1937
A pen outline of trees on a cliff top, seagulls above with etched colours for the foliage. The cliff edge and sea in the distance implied by shaded lines.
Colourways:
Orange ★★£
Pink ★★★££
Blue ★★★★£££

Bottom left:
Spire
Clarice Cliff
1937
A tree in the foreground, with a green and yellow hatching landscape behind, and on the horizon, house roofs and a church spire.
★★★★★££

Opposite:
Sunburst
Bizarre
1930
Very stylish star like motif surrounding and divided by triangles in yellow, orange and brown.
The design draws inspiration from the Aztec or Navajo cultures.
★★★★£££££

Top:
Umbrellas
Fantasque
1929-1930
The "umbrella" panels of the fuller *Umbrellas and Rain* design.
Colourways:
Orange ★★★£££
Red ★★★★££££

Bottom right:
Wedgwood invited "*Bizarre* Girl" Elsie Nixon back in 1993, and she recreated a limited edition of pieces in the *Delicia* design she had first done for Clarice in 1930.

studio. Norman recalls the very Dickensian atmosphere.

"*In those days you virtually touched your forelock when you approached the owner of the factory. Clarice was always reticent as far as her private life was concerned, always shying away from showing her true self, maybe not wanting to be friendly. Colley was always a headmaster kind of figure; what he said was absolute law. You never contradicted him, you were subservient. He was not unkind, but that was the way he was.*"

Norman Smith absorbed what was happening in the factory eagerly, touring the departments and learning from other staff, with an enthusiasm that echoed Clarice's in the Twenties. He recalls that hand-painting had virtually ceased, but Eileen Tharme did *Crocus* which Clara Thomas banded. *Biarritz* tableware shapes were still being produced. The factory could still export decorated goods to North and South America, Canada and Australia. Norman remembers that Peggy Davies was finally allowed to leave and was to become famous as a modeller for Royal Doulton, Betty Silvester also left around 1941. Then in 1942 the remaining staff were concentrated at Wilkinson's when the Newport Pottery site was taken over by the War Office. It was never to re-open.

Colley Shorter was 60 in 1942. His behaviour was at times eccentric, to save petrol he sometimes rode his horse into the works from Chetwynd. Against his wishes, his daughter Joan enrolled in the WAAF. She met a Canadian airman who she eventually married, and her moving to Canada was to greatly increase Colley's desire to export there after the war. As well as maintaining his routine at the factory, he enrolled in the Home Guard, although when he bought a full military uniform and wore it on duty the authorities objected.

Clarice Cliff-Shorter, as she now called herself, was 43 in 1942. There was soon little for her to do at the factory, so on many days she would stay at home as Colley went into work or did his shifts for the Home Guard. Her needs were attended to by the servants Bessy and Alice as Clarice found herself the mistress of Chetwynd House. Her love of Chetwynd was soon as great as Colley's and with the same determination she had shown in 1928, she set about her new life caring for him, the house, and the garden. Clarice exchanged *My Garden* for a real garden of over six acres. From the lounge at Chetwynd she could see a mass of roses, rhododendrons and hydrangeas, and the rockeries teemed with aubretia and gentians. It was to become her passion to the extent that she was never really to come out of retirement after the Second World War.

The story of A. J. Wilkinson's between 1946 and 1964 is not one of decline, on the contrary, Colley Shorter undertook a programme of modernisation that soon made it a showpiece factory. The bottle-ovens were demolished and replaced by gas-fired continuous ovens, new technology meant that many of the pre-war manual jobs were done mechanically. Clarice and Colley now had time to take breaks from the factory and spent Christmas 1949 in Canada. They visited Joan Shorter and her husband and combined this with a sales and promotional trip which resulted in newspaper coverage mentioning both Clarice Cliff and Colonel Shorter.

Restrictions on decorated ware for the home market, meant that the bulk of Wilkinson's production was of printed ware for export from 1946 until 1952, but Clarice installed Aubrey Dunn as decorating manager to re-establish a hand-painting shop. Hilda Lovatt contacted some of Clarice's old girls and hand-painting resumed on a small scale. Rene Dale, Winnie Pound, Florrie Winkle and Clara Thomas went back by 1946, Mary Moses joined in 1948 and Cissy Rhodes and Ethel Barrow in 1949. After sharing a room with lithographers for a while, a brand new *Bizarre* shop was established. This gave them a much more pleasant working environment than before the war and although they were now over thirty, around the factory they continued to be called the "*Bizarre* girls".

In 1947 Eric Grindley re-joined, he took a deep interest in the production methods in the factory. Naturally *Crocus* was as popular as ever, Eric recalls that the *My Garden* style was revived, and even *Rhodanthe*. However, changes in regulations for lead content in paint meant these were decorated in more subdued colours. The main production at this time was of *Georgian* shape dinnerware, with fine lining in gold and green, or gold and blue around the rim.

Bottom left:
Stroud
Bizarre
1933
A shoulder pattern of a cartouche with a cottage and tree motif against a band of colour. Colourways orange and green.
★★★££

Bottom right:
Trent
Bizarre
1937
A naturally coloured country scene with two tall trees in front of a short wooden bridge over an unseen brook, with flowers in the foreground.
★★★★£

Top:
Umbrellas & Rain
Fantasque
1929-1930
Two alternating abstract panels, one with stylised open umbrellas merging together, the other of rain symbolised as circles on a line.
Colourways:
Orange ★★★£££
Red ★★★★££££

Clarice's contributions were to be mainly supervisory, in 1951 she and Colley employed Eric Elliot, yet another young student from the Burslem School of Art, to act as designer. When restrictions on decorated ware were finally lifted in 1952, Clarice was a Director of Wilkinson's, the factory was finally able to produce decorated ware for the Home market. Lightning was not to strike twice though, the taste for printed patterns in overseas markets predominated. Clarice believed that by reviving old shapes the factory could pick up where it left off. This proved to be a mistake, and it was some time before it was realised, allowing competitors such as the Midwinter Pottery to gain a head start.

Eric Elliot's role in the factory was to take on greater importance when in October 1952 Clarice was rushed to hospital with stomach ulcers. She had been taking a herbal remedy for these, but not seeing a doctor. Colley Shorter was in London with Norman Smith, who remembers that as soon as Colley heard he dashed back to be with her.

Colley began to train Norman Smith to run overseas sales, which enabled him to spend more time with Clarice. At one stage this involved Norman joining them in North America. He recalled the arduous journey there in 1952.

"*Manchester Airport did not exist in those days. I took the train to London, then a four-engined plane to Shannon, from there to Iceland, Newfoundland to re-fuel, and on to Montreal. Colley was waiting and Clarice greeted me at the hotel, and we had dinner together that night. I was now becoming closer to Clarice and Colley, they made me part of their team, I had been chosen to take on Colley's mantle.*"

Norman toured Toronto and New York with them, securing orders for vitrified hotel ware and he recalls how Clarice designed patterns for hotel ware.

"*A pattern called Lily of the Valley designed for small plaques was now also to be applied to hotel ware. These were the thoughts going through her mind in 1953. The ideas were centred around putting printed designs onto existing shapes; she tried to marry shapes and*

Opposite:
Sunray (Night & Day)
Bizarre
1929-1930
Stylised black skyscrapers between panels of purple and orange sunrays, a bridge with stylised stars in the sky above, and a dark blue cloud.
Sunray Green is known from a few examples where the sunrays are orange and green.
★★★★£££££

This page:
Wax Flower
Bizarre
1930
Half a blue flower against black bars on an orange and honeyglaze ground.
★★★★★£££

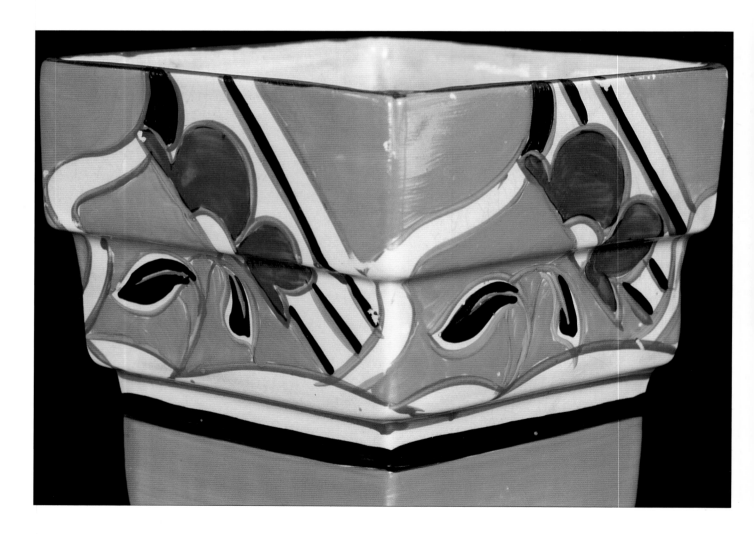

designs to give a new look. She was striving continually from a decorative point of view to bring these things to the fore."

The same year Clarice worked with Eric Elliot on designs that were to be completely or partly hand-painted. Having seen Clarice's archives he used bold colours for patterns such as *Sunkissed*, *Lavender Lily* and *Magnolia*, but these were purely a sideline in the factory which was dominated by printed or lithographed decoration. Other new lines included a revival of the pre-war *Windsor* shape in two-tone glazes of grey with either pink, blue or green. A stylish range called *Novota*, was produced but judging by rarity now, did not sell in any quantity. The *Conical* bowl was briefly revived but decorated with a printed design of a rose it looked incongruous.

Despite their love of the Potteries, Clarice and Colley soon realised that they preferred to spend time with each other rather than at the factory they had shared since the Twenties. They undertook a series of exciting long holidays, sometimes combined with trips to overseas agents. These trips were to dominate the years from 1952 to 1958. One itinerary involved staying with friends in Bermuda, then going to Los Angeles. From there they went on to Canada to see Joan, then they made the return trip on a Cunard Liner from New York. A European trip in one of Colley's Rolls-Royces started in Paris, then saw them chauffeured through Italy, stopping at Florence, Casino, Sienna, Sorrento, Rome, Capri and Venice.

Between holidays Clarice did attempt to work on new lines, in 1955 and 1956 more modern ware was introduced including the *Lynton Coupe* dinnerware, followed by the *Devon* shape. However, the introduction of a thirty percent sales tax on Home sales did not encourage Clarice and Colley to persevere with these in the competitive Home market.

By 1958 Colley Shorter was 76 years old, his health began to fail, so their holidays were limited to England. They toured in Devon, Cornwall and Dorset, ambling along the beaches, or visiting gardens and stately homes together. Often they would just spend their time enjoying Chetwynd House where Clarice was always in the

Opposite bottom:
Twin Peaks
Bizarre
1929
A landscape outlined in purple, with two red mountains, a blue lake and orange trees.
Known from one piece that appears to be a sample. Photograph shows front and reverse.
★★★★★£££

Opposite top:
Windflowers
Bizarre
1933-1934
Known from just one example on an eighteen inch charger. A circle of yellow, blue and brown freehand flowers with pale green leaves, surrounds a brown *Cafe-au-Lait* ground.
This design can only be dated stylistically as there are no clues to the exact date.
★★★★★£££

This page:
Woman's Journal
Bizarre
1931
A printed floral motif enamelled in orange, green, blue and red, with yellow and orange banding. This was a tableware design offered exclusively to readers of Woman's Journal magazine on a mail-order basis, hence the name.
★★★££

garden, Colley wandered in the orchard. Norman Smith was now a friend as well as an employee and occasionally they invited him to join them on summer days.

"*Clarice was a very keen gardener, she loved plants, the garden was covered in hydrangeas and roses. They also had this small field they cultivated, they hired a machine to cut the hay and really enjoyed this. Colley would come in with a basket of crab apples from his orchard and hand them out, or Clarice would come in with tales of the pet goose chasing them. We would sit in the window seat looking down the garden and discuss the factory. Clarice would ask about my childhood, what I had done, my parents. We would talk about the days events and it almost became a works meeting. Sometimes Clarice would pull open drawers and show me the collection of potlids. On another occasion she showed me the dining table she had decorated with the help of one of her nieces while Colley was away in Canada. Then she'd say, 'Colley its a quarter to seven', so the radio was turned on for The Archer's and we kept quiet until it finished, and then we started chatting again.*"

In 1961 a small feature on hand-painting in *Pottery Gazette & Glass Trade Review* showed Cissy Rhodes, Florrie Winkle and Ethel Barrow, the last of the *Bizarre* girls, decorating *Crocus* at Wilkinson's. The same year Norman Smith undertook massive overseas selling trips, going to America, Australia and New Zealand. It was during such a trip in 1963 that Norman felt uneasy, so cut short his last few days to return early.

"*I flew back and arrived at midday, rested an hour, then drove over to Chetwynd House. The maid let me in, I walked into the square hall with the balustrade running round, just as Clarice walked down the stairs, and said, 'Norman, you're just too late', Colley had died just half-an-hour before.*"

Without Colley Shorter, neither Wilkinson's nor Clarice could carry on. She had no heart to work again at the factory and accepted an offer from Roy Midwinter of Midwinter Pottery to buy the works. Paintress Cissy Rhodes recalled how she found

Opposite:
Summerhouse
Fantasque
1931-1933
A red hut, a tree with green trunk and pendulous yellow foliage, black bushes, and a blue lake. Although banding colours vary, the only slight variation to the design is that occasionally the hut roof is orange.
★★★★££££

This page:
Woodland
Bizarre
1931
A printed outline with enamelling of blue and purple flowers, with a tree behind with orange and green foliage. This was Wilkinson's pattern 8869 but was issued with *Clarice Cliff* markings.
The Wilkinson's number indicates this was perhaps done there as a way of producing Bizarre ware without having the time consuming outlining stage.
★★★£££

212 R

out that the factory was to be sold.

Opposite:
Windbells
Fantasque
1933-1934
A tree with a curving black trunk and blue lenticular foliage, against wavy blue, green and yellow striped background.
★★★£££

"*Miss Cliff came and told us in 1964 that she was finishing, and that she had sold the business to Midwinter's on condition that they took us all on. For a while she kept on coming round, and strangely when she was ill, Mr. Walker who had set me on in 1926 came back briefly to look after us. He said, 'I remember you' and talked of taking me on. We did not have a party when Miss Cliff left as of the original girls there was only myself and Florrie Winkle. I finally left in August 1968 when I was given just 28 days notice having done 37 years.*"

The rediscovery of Clarice Cliff's work began just a few years after the factory closed. From the late Sixties until the present day has been a time of constant surprises, as each year new designs and shapes appeared. Unlike most other collectibles, there was an endless supply of fresh pieces. In the late Sixties collectors in the Brighton area were able to buy *Inspiration* vases for £6 and a collector in Bath bought an *Age of Jazz* figure for £20, when a typical bedsit cost £4.50 a week.

A major collector, Martin Battersby, was the first writer to draw attention to Clarice Cliff pottery. In 1969 in his book *Decorative Thirties* he illustrated her work with a new colour photograph of a *Delecia Stamford* teapot, a *Broth* candlestick and a *House & Bridge* bowl.

Although some of the interest in the *Bizarre* years was percolating back to her, Clarice ignored this. She preferred to spend her time looking after Colley's things, speaking to her sister Ethel nightly on the telephone and occasionally exchanging letters with Hilda Lovatt. Clarice's priority was her garden, where Reg Lamb her claymaker from 1919 was now her helper. On wet days she stayed indoors cleaning the valuable antiques that filled Chetwynd House. These became a worrying responsibility as they were only in her care. Colley Shorter had left them to Joan after Clarice's death.

She was still fond of all her old staff but was remote from them. However, when she heard that one worker was seriously ill she paid for her and her husband to stay at Rhos-on-Sea for two weeks. She called *Bizarre* girl Mary Brown to make the arrangements, but swore her to secrecy over who had paid. Occasionally Clarice would drive across to Newcastle-under-Lyme to shop. It was on one of these days that she met Marjory Higginson who recalled that Clarice was still as smartly dressed as the day she had first met her in 1928. Clarice talked in an animated fashion about the *Bizarre* years, and how nice it was when things were going well. She told Marjory she had seen some of the other girls during her shopping trips. Marjory got the impression that Clarice was rather isolated and perhaps lost, with the two most important things in her life, Colley and the pottery - gone.

Clarice Cliff was acknowledged as a major Art Deco designer in 1971 by the *Minneapolis Institute of Arts* when a large number of her pieces were included in their influential *World of Art Deco* exhibition. Later the same year in Britain, Martin Battersby and other enthusiasts, planned the first exhibition of just Clarice Cliff ware at the Brighton Museum and Art Gallery. The curator Betty O'Loony needed some factual information to compile the catalogue and called an expert on *Bizarre* - Clarice Cliff. It was amazing that she even got through to Clarice, who had a "ringing code" only known to her sisters and a few friends so she was able to ignore all other calls. Clarice found the time she had to spend writing notes annoying, ill-health and a failing memory meant the material she sent contributed little knowledge about the ware. Luckily, the pottery spoke for itself and one hundred pieces were displayed from January 15th to February 20th in 1972. Clarice did not visit the exhibition or tell her family about it until it closed. The catalogue was just a few duplicated sheets, but a silk-screen poster by Martin Battersby of a Thirties woman embracing a *Melon* vase, has become as collectable as the ware it publicised.

In October 1972, within eight months of the exhibition closing, Clarice Cliff died at Chetwynd House. She was found by Reg Lamb, her gardener, sitting in her favourite chair, listening to the radio.

CHAPTER II

1973

THE COLLECTORS

In December 1972 *Art & Antiques* magazine published a long article about Clarice Cliff and *Bizarre*. It was written by an early collector of her work, Graham Crossingham-Gower.

"*Vitality, originality and style are words usually applied to the artist and his canvas rather than to the ceramic designer and decorator. Yet these words must surely join with those of dynamic individualism to describe fully the work of Clarice Cliff, whose pottery is at last gaining recognition as being truly representative of the Art Deco period.*"

His insight at the time was amazing, there was no study of designs or shapes for him to refer to, he had clearly learnt by collecting ware.

"*Conical casters offer the collector an interesting aspect of her work as the same pattern (shape) can be found decorated in many ways. Prices range from £2 to £8.*" An Autumn plate was prophetically captioned, "*An excellent example of Clarice Cliff's balanced use of colour - it dates from about 1930. Today's value is about £12 - a cheerful investment indeed.*"

The *L'Odeon* shop, near King's Road in London, established itself as one of the main locations to buy *Bizarre*. Flamboyant owner Nöel Tovey displayed it in tall, lit cabinets that added to its allure, and spread *Yo Yo* vases, *Bon Bon* sets, and complete teasets out on Alvar Aalto tables. The result was that more collectors saw it and loved it. As many other dealers in Twentieth century collectables became aware of Clarice

Opposite:
Windmill
Appliqué
1930-1931
A dark blue windmill by a river against a cloudy red and orange sky and a green and black wood.
★★★★★£££££

This page:
Xanthic (Harbour Scene)
Bizarre
1932-1933
An abstract design with grey, yellow and orange panels sharing elements of the earlier *Orange 'V'* design.
Seen by some as an abstract harbour scene.
★★★★£££

Cliff, more and more of the shops on King's Road, and stalls at Portobello Market had pieces. These were often sources of bargains as the dealers knew good pieces of 'Cliff' when they saw them, but often undervalued them as they did not realise how rare they were.

Clarice Cliff's ware was then discovered by collectors in America and Canada. It had never been marketed there in any quantity until after the *Bizarre* and *Fantasque* ranges had been discontinued, so there was no source. North Americans holidaying in Britain were drawn by the bright colours and geometric shapes, and this inevitably led to prices increasing for major pieces. Soon, galleries and private dealers were selling the ware in America. The natural supply of the ware in Australia and New Zealand, where it had been exported throughout the Thirties meant there were soon enthusiasts there also.

The endeavours of two enthusiastic collectors, Peter Wentworth-Shields and Kay Johnson to write the first book, *Clarice Cliff*, resulted in a charming work issued under the auspices of *L'Odeon* in 1976. It motivated a whole new army of *Bizarre* collectors. The book was linked to an impressive exhibition held at the *L'Odeon* shop featured in colour in the centre-pages of *Art & Antiques*. The first edition of 1510 copies of the book sold-out and was then unavailable which further fuelled interest.

The acceleration of interest in Clarice Cliff in the Eighties was first celebrated with an exhibition at the gallery of the Crafts Council of Australia in Sydney. This drew more collectors from both Australia and New Zealand to her work. A sheet circulated to British antique centres in 1981, led to the formation of the Clarice Cliff Collectors Club in 1982.

In June 1983 Christie's, London, staged an auction solely of Clarice Cliff pottery. This was unprecedented, but then again so was the pottery. As the large crowds assembled for the evening auction, individuals who previously thought that only they and a few friends loved 'Clarice', were shocked to see not dozens but hundreds of other enthusiasts.

This page:
Xavier
Bizarre
1932-1934
An abstract freehand panel between *Cafe-au-Lait* similar to the earlier *Xanthic* pattern.
★★★★£££

Opposite:
Yugoslavian Dancers
Bizarre
1933-1934
Known from just one eighteen inch flat plaque, this is the most elaborate design issued in the *Bizarre* range. A pair of dancers in peasant costumes are surrounded by motifs of mountains and flowers in *Latona* and *Appliqué* style, in over 20 colours. Possibly done for an exhibition as a centre piece. It is probably the work of Fred Ridgway or perhaps John Butler. *In the Christie's 8th November 1984 sale this plaque sold for £9616 which was a record price at that time.*

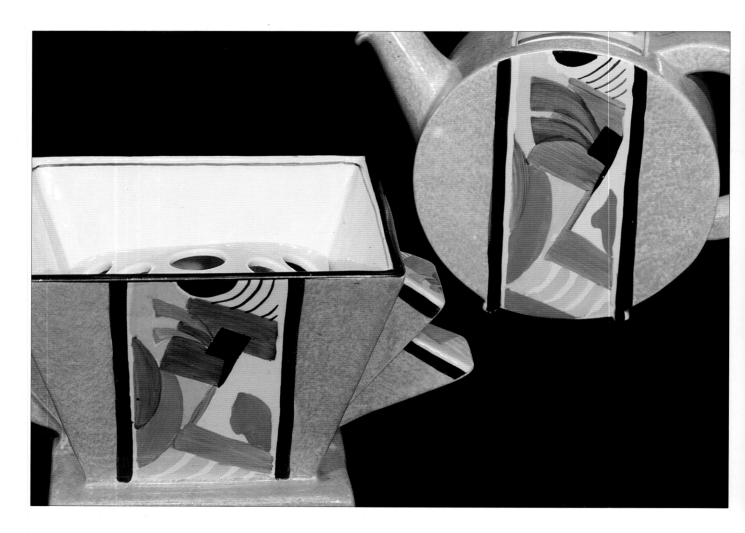

As awareness was stirred by post-auction publicity, so demand was satiated as people realised they actually owned some of the pottery, put it into auction, or sold it to dealers. A mass of new designs and shapes appeared, again stimulating further interest from existing and new collectors.

Midwinter, the company who had taken over Newport Pottery and Wilkinson's site decided to reproduce Clarice Cliff ware in 1985. Many collectors predicted this would bring about the end of collecting. On their *Stonehenge* tableware shape they reproduced *Melon, Crocus*, and *Oranges & Lemons* as a full colour print. Ironically, in a ceramic déjà-vu, a limited edition series was painted freehand and they took on sixteen-year old trainees to decorate this. Gradually a *Honolulu* shape 14, *Summerhouse* plaque, six *Conical* sugar dredgers and a *Conical* bowl in *Umbrellas & Rain* started to be delivered to those who had ordered them. The limited edition was not complete, however, before the factory ignominiously closed as it was absorbed by Wedgwood.

The publication of the book *The Bizarre Affair* in May 1988, gave collectors a comprehensive understanding of the ware for the first time. In America there was extensive coverage in *Vogue* and the *New York Times* in Britain *Homes & Gardens* put Clarice on its cover, as countless other newspapers and magazines around the world could not resist doing full-colour features. A mass of new collectors were exposed to *Bizarre* in all its colour, and inevitably in the following months prices sky-rocketed.

A further book, *Collecting Clarice Cliff* added to the impetus, and by 1989 realising how interest had grown, *Christie's* reflected this by holding all Clarice Cliff auctions in March and November. The November auction then became established as an annual event.

In the Nineties a mass of events celebrated Clarice Cliff: spontaneous exhibitions were held in London in 1990, Manchester in 1993, Holland in 1994 and Hampshire in 1995. Wedgwood issued two sets of reproductions of her work.

For some time the Meisel's in New York had sold mainly Clarice Cliff pottery from one of their galleries in SoHo, but the first all Clarice Cliff shop in Britain, *Rich Designs*, was opened in Stratford upon Avon by *Bizarre* Girls Elsie Nixon and Rene Dale in 1992.

Fewer new patterns are being unearthed each year, now that the flood of the early Eighties has turned into a trickle. But as you will see on the next two pages there are always a few surprises! Some of these patterns are completely new, whilst others are unique colour variations of more familiar examples.

The pottery has become much more difficult to obtain, so collectors have come to rely on a relationship with a dealer to obtain 'special' pieces for their collections. We hope that the dealers featured over the next few pages will help you to find your dream piece.

It is after all, the collectors who will ensure that Clarice Cliff and her pottery go from strength to strength and her importance is fully appreciated. However, it may take the 1999 Clarice Cliff Centenary Exhibitions and the start of the Twenty First Century to put her work truly into perspective.

Bottom left:
Watermill
Bizarre
1930
Unique at present this design is perhaps an adaptation of *Sunray*.
★★★★£££

Bottom right:
Winsome
Bizarre
1929
A complicated series of abstract shapes painted in various colours. One of the many variations of designs after the *Original Bizarre* triangles.
★★★★£££

Top:
Zap
Bizarre
1930
An orange circle with a yellow stepped centre below a blue and white arch, on the reverse an orange flower with green leaves.
★★★★★££££

Top left:
Crazy Paving
Bizarre
1930
An unusual design known from three pieces.
★★★★★£££

Top right:
Posy
Bizarre
1930
Known from two examples, this design was executed on an experimental glaze which looks like a 'crumbly' Latona.
Probably the inspiration for Nemesia.
★★★★★££

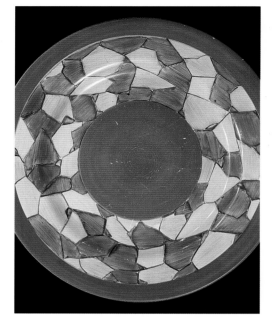
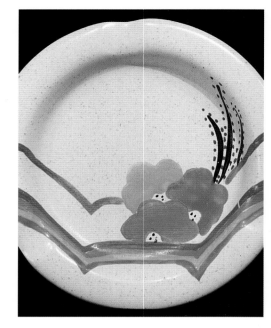

Middle left:
Orange Roof Cottage
Fantasque
1932-1933
This variation known from one example, has the roof painted yellow, the side wall orange and the gable wall green. The rest of the pattern is "standard".
It was probably produced as a sample piece before full production started. It certainly appears to be experimental as the outline is executed with a fine brush and the enamelling seems "too careful".
See also page 156.

Middle right:
Crab Apple
Bizarre
1931
Known from just this example on the rare 401 shape rose bowl. The design is hand painted fruit and leaves.
★★★★★££

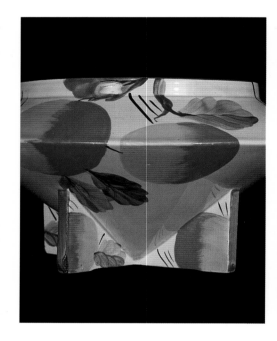

Bottom left:
Sand Flower
Bizarre
1930
An orange centre surrounded by large orange flowers next to smaller blue flowers.
The date mark on the plate indicates it was contemporary with Gayday.
★★★★★££

Bottom right:
Mango
Bizarre
1931
Orange, double skinned fruit with bold black leaves, only found so far on a brown *Cafe-au-Lait* background.
★★★★£££

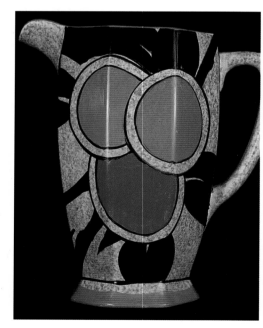

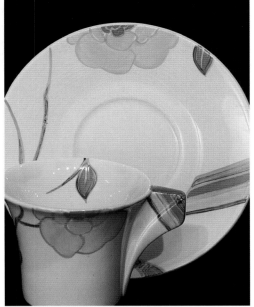

Top left:
Scarlet Flower
Bizarre
1930
Large red flower with green leaves and tracing over the entire piece. Mostly seen on plates and biscuit barrels with EPNS lids and handles.
★★★★££

Top right:
Yellow Rose
Bizarre
1932
This edge design is known only on tableware at present. It features a flower with yellow and tan petals and a spindly stem.
★★★★£

Middle left:
Marlow
Bizarre
1933
This design is unique in that it combines many of Clarice's painting techniques. The flowers are a lithograph and are then hand painted. The background is aerographed and the yellow etched.
★★★★★££

Middle right:
Waterlily
Bizarre
1931
This design features many elements from *Chintz* and may have been a forerunner of the pattern. The flowers are in yellow, the leaves green.
★★★★£££

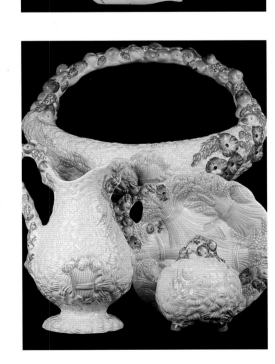

Bottom left:
Picasso Flower
Bizarre
1930
A blue example of the more familiar red version.
★★★★★£££
See also page 166.

Bottom right:
Celtic Harvest
Clarice Cliff
1936
Rare pink glaze examples.
★★★££
See also page 62.

MUIR HEWITT
ART DECO ORIGINALS

*A*n old children's annual with designs by British illustrator Anne Anderson, which was handed down to me, was initially behind my love of the flowing, linear style of much English Art Deco pottery and in particular the work of Clarice Cliff. Anne Anderson's sinuous lines and simplified stylised work led me on to an interest in the pre-war work of Walt Disney which was influenced by the work of European artists and illustrators.

Here are a few favourite pieces from my collection.

A Christmas present of Dan Klein's book on Art Deco, given to me by a favourite uncle and aunt when I was seventeen, intensified my interest in the period. Four years later, whilst at college in Wolverhampton, studying for my Graphic Design degree, I saw the Disney-esque *House and Bridge* design poster for the first Clarice Cliff book published by *L'Odeon* which became the catalyst for my enduring passion for all aspects of Art Deco and my every spare moment was spent searching for pieces of pottery from this era. Eventually my obsession became my occupation when thirteen years ago I opened my shop at the Halifax Antiques Centre.

MUIR HEWITT • ART DECO ORIGINALS

at Halifax Antiques Centre, Queens Road Mills, Queens Road/Gibbet Street, Halifax HX1 4LR

Open Tuesday to Saturday, 10am to 5pm.

The shop has a wide selection of ceramics by Clarice Cliff, Susie Cooper, Charlotte Rhead and others. The stock also includes an ever changing selection of mirrors, lighting and small furniture from the 1920's to the 1950's.

For further details please telephone or fax on **01422 347377**. Evenings Tel: **01274 882051**

Opposite, some pieces of Clarice Cliff pottery from my current stock at the time of publication.
On the wall, a portrait by Jane Lewis, friend and painter.
The portrait hung in the National Portrait Gallery for the summer of 1991, when Jane was one of 60 finalists in the British Petroleum portrait awards.

Jane Lewis,
The Portal Gallery,
16a Grafton Street,
London W1X 3LF
Tel: **0171 629 3506**

Photography by **Keith Paisley**. Tel: **01830 520035**

Antiques on the Square are easy to find in the heart of the West Midlands at Church Stretton, Shropshire. We are in the centre of town, just off the A49.

Our impressive display contains a wide and constantly changing selection of *Clarice Cliff* with over two hundred rare and interesting pieces always available. Enthusiasts will be truly fascinated by this very unique gallery which is *open six days* a week or by appointment.

Collectors old and new are very welcome at our shop where *specialist advice* is freely given by Chris Radford and his well informed team. All items are photographed for postal enquiries and research is undertaken.

CHRIS RADFORD
ANTIQUES ON THE SQUARE
INCORPORATING
CENTRAL ANTIQUE COURIERS

Sandford Avenue, Church Stretton, Shropshire, SY6 6BH, U.K.

Telephone:01694.724111 (Gallery)   01694.723072 (Residence 1)   01694.723985 (Residence 2)

Fax (1): 01694.724138   Fax (2): 01214.226606   Mobile Tel: 0831.336052

BANANA DANCE

Long established specialists, offering one of the largest selections of top quality Clarice Cliff in the country.

We offer a personal service and advice on collection building, restoration, repairs, and insurance valuations.

We'll buy or sell single items or whole collections and offer a wedding list service for Clarice Cliff, Susie Cooper, Shelley, Charlotte Rhead, Ducal/Burleighware.

See us at Loughborough. Alexandra Palace. Battersea. Warwick. Newark and Ardingly Fairs.

BANANA DANCE Unit 20, Northcote Rd Antiques, 155a Northcote Rd., Battersea London SW11.

Or contact Jonathan Daltrey direct- telephone or fax 0181 699 7728 anytime.

Suppliers to the trade worldwide.

> *"We offer a very large selection of Clarice Cliff pottery, displayed in our new custom renovated building, in Stratford upon Avon."*

Des Jones and Richard Green had both been collecting Clarice Cliff for several years when they decided to form Rich Designs and specialise in selling Clarice Cliff pottery. They began from a small stall in an antiques market, opening the first all Clarice Cliff shop two years later.

They have recently completed refurbishing their new custom building - Gallery One - in Stratford upon Avon.

> *"Our aim is to provide the very best selection of designs, in all price ranges, to accommodate every collector worldwide. We would be happy to assist in building your collection, especially if you are searching for that 'impossible piece'.*
>
> *We offer secure shipping facilities worldwide as well as a fully comprehensive valuation service."*

...Always buy what you like...

RICH DESIGNS *at* GALLERY ONE

1 Shakespeare Street, Stratford upon Avon,
Warwickshire CV37 6RN
Tel: 01789 261612 (Shop)   Fax: 01789 772444
Tel: 01789 772111 (Office)

Part of a collection of *Appliqué* pieces we have helped a collector amass over the past two years.

Acacia
Bizarre
1932
A name in the 1932 order book, of a pattern with a large and small tree, no other details.

Arizona
Clarice Cliff
1937
An abstract semi-circular motif and parallel line.

Aura
Clarice Cliff
1936
Etching across the rim of tableware, or the edge of teaware, Colourways green and yellow.

Batanga
1928
A simple design of stylised flowers forming two garlands around a plate, printed and then enamelled. This has Wilkinson's marks, and is believed to be the work of Dolly Cliff.
★★★££

Beechwood
Clarice Cliff
1936
A creamy matt glaze with a partial decoration of a twig, with leaves in shades of brown.
★★£

Braidwood
Sample
1935-1936
A floral design of powder blue cornflowers with green leaves, above geometric hatching in blue and green.
Known from one example discovered in Australia.
★★★★★££

Cherry Tree
Clarice Cliff
1937
A range of shapes with an embossed tree with lilac coloured fruit, on a matt mushroom glaze.
★★£

Chestnut
Clarice Cliff
1937-1938
A range of shapes with embossed leaves in natural shades, on a matt mushroom glaze.
★★£

Clematis
Clarice Cliff
1937
A motif of Clematis flowers.

Cornwall
Bizarre
1933
A tree in a stylised garden in shades of green. The rarest colourway of *Moonlight*.
★★★★★£££

Cruiseware
Bizarre
1936
Stylish designs of people in scenes on a 1930's Cruise liner, produced with lithographed outline with painted detail, produced on amoebic shaped saucers to hold a teacup and biscuits.
The saucer shape pre-dates the Coupe style that was to predominate in the Fifties.

Delecia Peaches
Bizarre
1933-1934
Very similar to *Delecia Citrus* but easily distinguished as the leaves are just green, and the fruit has a crescent shape to the right.
★★★★★£££

Dijon
Clarice Cliff
1936
A name in the 1936 order book.

Dolphins
Clarice Cliff
1935
A shoulder design of dolphins painted in red.
★★★★£

Exotic
Clarice Cliff
1936
A shoulder pattern of leaves and gold lines.
★★★£

Florida
1930
An outline floral print motif, with hand enamelled flowers, known on tableware and coffee-sets, possibly a pre-Clarice Cliff Newport Pottery design.
★★★★£

Foam
1929-1930
This was probably produced for the overseas Art Pottery market, shortly before or as *Bizarre* began, some examples have a J. Butler signature on them.
★★★★££

Forest Leaves
1932
Large freehand naturally coloured leaves on a branch.
★★★££

Fuchsia
Clarice Cliff
1929
Red and blue flowers as a motif on tableware, an old Newport Pottery design still in production occasionally in the early Thirties.
★★★£

Gallion
1936
Name of an unknown design, possibly for tableware.

Gloria Crocus
1931
Underglaze flowers in dull pastel colours.
★★★★££

Golden Oranges
Sample
1929
A design known only in the factory sample books at present, but its presence there as a finished water-colour indicates it was definitely produced. Oranges with gold leaves, against grey and black bars criss-crossing underneath.
Probably contemporary with Geometric Flowers.

Gordon
Bizarre
1935
Blue, green, and beige banding on tableware.
★£

Grill
Tableware
1934
An 'L' shaped motif with stylised flowers around it, only known at present from a drawing in the pattern book.

Hawthorn
Tableware
1936
A motif of hawthorn leaves and berries, blue and orange colourways.
★★£

Hello
Bizarre
1933
Spots randomly dotted on tea and tableware, produced in several colours and colourways.
★★★£

Indian Summer
1929-1931
A landscape and tree design produced as a coloured print with enamelled yellow and orange on. Known with a Wilkinson's mark. It was probably done in Clarice Cliff's style and sold at a cheaper price than *Bizarre*.

Inspiration Delphinium
1931
Tall flowers in blue, purple, pink and yellow, against black, by a decorative background.
★★★★££££

Inspiration Embossed
1929
Old Newport Pottery shapes, with Victorian style raised motifs and *Inspiration* glaze applied to the surface.
★★★★£

Inspiration Garden
1931
A tree with brown trunk in a garden with small flowers.
★★★★££££

Inspiration Nasturtium
1930
The standard *Nasturtium* design in *Inspiration* blue, purple and pink.
★★★★££££

Jagged Flower
Bizarre
1931
Possibly a pattern from the *Nuage* range but only known from one example.

Kang
Clarice Cliff
1935
Ware with simple abstract embossed shapes, covered in grey glaze, possibly old Newport Pottery stock rejuvenated.
★★★★££

Kensington
Clarice Cliff
1936
A *Biarritz* tableware design of stylised tulips drawn in outline, with geometric hatching through them.

Latona Aztec
Latona
1929-1930
Purple and lilac sunburst, above a yellow line ascending in steps either side.
Known from one Dover jardiniere.
★★★★★£££

Latona Blossom
Latona
1929
Clematis flowers in purple and red with black leaves.
The same design was produced on a trellis as part of the Appliqué range.
★★★★£££

Latona Brown
1929-1930
A version of the glaze with a pale brown colour, which seems to have been prone to 'gobbing'.
This is probably why it was only produced briefly, but it could theoretically be found in any of the late 1929, or early 1930 Latona designs.
★★★★£££

Latona Cartoon Flowers
Latona
1930
Amoeba shaped flowers with purple flowing colour beneath, and black diagonal lines to one side.
★★★★£££

Latona Geometric
Latona
1929
A simple edge decoration on ware, of 'dog tooth' triangles coloured in purple and orange, and other colours.
This was the earliest design used on the Latona glaze.
★★★★★£££

Latona Knight Errant
Latona
1930-1931
A knight on horseback by a wall, with details in red and silver.
Designed by John Butler as early as 1926, he painted it above the fireplace in the inglenook at Chetwynd for Colley Shorter.
The same design was produced on Inspiration ware.
★★★★★£££££

Latona Stained Glass
Latona
1929-1930
Angular lines covering the ware, some coloured to form a motif.
★★★£££

Milano
1935
A range of ware with the shape partly ribbed, partly smooth with simple broad bands of one or two colours.
★★★★★£

Morning
Clarice Cliff
1935
A simple variation of the *Rhodanthe* design, with flowers floating amidst a band of fine lines covering the ware.
★★★★£

Ophelia
Clarice Cliff
1938-1941 and post war
An outline print in brown of flowers in a basket, hand-painted in enamel colours.
★★★£

Palm
Bizarre
1934
A stylised tree with grass around the base.
★★★★★£££

Patina Blue Firs
Bizarre
1933-1934
The *Blue Firs* design on the *Patina* ground.
★★★★£££

Patina Coastal
Bizarre
1932-1933
A brown, green and yellow tree by a simple coast.
★★★★£££

Patina Country
Bizarre
1932-1933
A rolling landscape painted freehand with a small fountain scratched out of the paint.
★★★★£££

Patina Daisy
Bizarre
1932-1933
Blue, pink and purple daisies with yellow centres.
★★★★££

Piccadilly
Clarice Cliff
1935
A simple floral motif for *Biarritz* tableware.
★★★★£

Raffia
Clarice Cliff
1936-1937
A large range of ware with surface modelling resembling woven raffia.
Variations Raffia Floral and Raffia Indiana (colours unknown).
★★£

Rainbow
Clarice Cliff
1934
A large blue and green band around ware, with a small insert of red, orange and yellow banding.
★★£

Regatta
1929-1930
A design by John Butler with a distant sea with colourful yachts on, and the coast and trees in the foreground, using mixture of *Inspiration* underglaze techniques, and on-glaze enamelling.
This was probably produced for the overseas Art Pottery market, shortly before or as Bizarre began, some examples have a J. Butler signature on them.
★★★££

Reverie
Clarice Cliff
1935
Wavy lines, dot clusters and a stroke of colour as a motif on tableware.
★★★£

Spring Crocus
1933-1963
Pink, yellow and blue flowers.
★★★££

Springtime
1932-1934
Tableware motif of *Crocus* flowers above a wavy line.
This is confusingly referred to as Peter Pan Crocus in factory literature.
★★★££

Summer
1934-1935
The name of a pale green translucent apple coloured glaze on which adaptations of standard designs were painted.
Examples known are Summer Nasturtium and Summer Crocus.
★★★★£

Tahiti
1929-1930
A range of ware produced with underglaze blue and on-glaze enamel decoration, credited to Len Allen whose signature is on some pieces.
Nothing is known of this designer, but the shapes the design are found in imply a date of 1928 or 1929.
★★★★££

Tibetan
Pre 1928
Runnings in lustre outlined in gold on old Wilkinson's shapes. A John Butler range that Clarice Cliff worked on and eventually pieces were issued with a *Clarice Cliff* mark.

Twig
Clarice Cliff
1936
A twig forming a small motif on the ware.
★★£

Vienna
Clarice Cliff
1936
A simple design of finely executed dots and banding on *Biarritz* tableware.
★★£

Wheat
Bizarre
1931
A print of ears of wheat with hand-painted colour. Newport pattern number 6485.
★★£

Windows
Bizarre
1929
A simple pattern of overlapping oblongs in black outline with sections coloured in orange, yellow or black.
Known from one example.
★★★★★£££

Yellow Orchid
Bizarre
1934-1935
A floral design with aerographed orange over whole of ware, except for the outline of the flower which was hand-painted after aerographing.
Probably an experimental piece, this is at present unique, and the marks indicate a date of 1934 to 1935.

Yoo Hoo
Tableware
1930-1931
Ware painted all over in red and black, generally with red feet or handles and black body.
The backstamps indicate this was probably decorated at Wilkinson's as the black was aerographed.
★★★££

Yuan
Clarice Cliff
1937
Two cottages and two trees painted freehand as a motif on vases, generally on a green glazed background.
★★★★£

FURTHER READING

Clarice Cliff
Kay Johnson &
Peter Wentworth-Shields
L'Odeon 1976

Clarice Cliff - The Bizarre Affair
Leonard Griffin,
Louis & Susan Pear Meisel
Thames & Hudson 1988

Collecting Clarice Cliff
Howard Watson
Kevin Francis Publishing 1988

The Shorter Connection
Irene & Gordon Hopwood
Richard Dennis Publications 1992

Shelley Potteries
Watkins, Harvey, Senft
Barrie & Jenkins 1980

The Decorative Thirties
Martin Battersby
Studio Vista 1969

The World of Art Deco
Bevis Hillier
Minneapolis Institute of Arts 1971

Missuses & Mould runners
Jacqueline Sarsby
Open University Press

Art & Antiques
Independent Magazines 1972

**The Reviews of the Clarice Cliff
Collectors Club**
Leonard R. Griffin
C.C.C.C. from 1982 onwards

**Clarice Cliff auction catalogues
from 1983 onwards**
Christie's South Kensington

Thirties (Exhibition catalogue)
Arts Council 1980

**Susie Cooper Productions
(Exhibition catalogue)**
Ann Eatwell
Victoria & Albert Museum 1987

Clarice Cliff (Exhibition catalogue)
Paul Kopocek
Decorative Arts Group, London 1990

Greta Pottery
Pat Halfpenny
*Journal of the Northern Ceramics Society
Volume 8 1991*